The African
in
the mirror

Books by the same author

Cyclones of the Human Heart (Janus Publishing Company, 2001)
The Shadow of Rainbow   (Tomio Publishing House, 2003)
The Children of Signatures   (iUniverse, Inc., 2004)

The African in the mirror

◆

A Critical Appraisal of the Past and Present Role of Africans and African Religiosity in the Development Crisis of Sub-Sahara Africa.

Abimbola Lagunju

iUniverse, Inc.
New York Lincoln Shanghai

The African in the mirror

A Critical Appraisal of the Past and Present Role of Africans and African Religiosity in the Development Crisis of Sub-Sahara Africa.

iUniverse books may be ordered through booksellers or by contacting:

iUniverse
2021 Pine Lake Road, Suite 100
Lincoln, NE 68512
www.iuniverse.com
1-800-Authors (1-800-288-4677)

ISBN-13: 978-0-595-34819-0 (pbk)
ISBN-13: 978-0-595-79549-9 (ebk)
ISBN-10: 0-595-34819-X (pbk)
ISBN-10: 0-595-79549-8 (ebk)

Printed in the United States of America

For Rachael Morohunmubo Lagunju (1938–2005) who showed the way by example.

Contents

My Words

I am not a philosopher, neither a sociologist, nor a historian. And certainly not a politician. I am also not a specialist on Africa. I am the common African man, who feels burdened by the consequences of African history, lives the pain of the humiliations of its present, and has a great concern for its future.

My question is simple: What has made us black Africans so vulnerable and susceptible that we, the black race, are at the receiving end of all humanity's disasters? We have always been told that others have been and are the drivers of our destiny while we have been non-complacent but compliant passengers down a road, the destination of which is unknown to us. We have chosen to underemphasize our role in the mishandling of our past and present. We appear to have resigned ourselves to being guided politically, economically and more recently culturally by alien standards and have conveniently ignored to find more suitable home-grown alternatives to the manner of existence handed down to us.

I have moved freely between the landmarks of African political history and experiences over the last eight hundred years and I have tried to condense my views into this small book. In writing the book, I made a conscious effort not to dwell on the intricacies of "*the how*" of the historical landmarks that shaped the course of African history. These are well known and documented. Rather I tried to look at the role of the African, both as subject and object in the events that led to these landmarks and how much the African has learned from these experiences.

I have not sought to question the motive of people from other cultures with whom the African has had contact and the benefits that the former have reaped through this contact. I have questioned the motive of the African in allowing this to happen. I have sought to understand if the negative experiences derived from these contacts have in any way been taken into serious consideration by Africans in charting the course of Africa's destiny. Other cultures that have been subjected to lesser atrocities than Africa in their history chant "Never Again!" as a political philosophy and as a fact of life.

My question is what does Africa chant?

In the mind of many, even some on the geographical entity called Africa, the term African means *Black African*. Taking this cue, and also convinced that the historical experiences of Black Africans are different from those of non-black Africans, I have used the term Africa in the book to refer only to black Sub-Sahara Africa. And the term African refers to Black Africans.

The contents of this book express the views of a common man and are not intended as material for mind-bending academic analysis. The book is directed at today's African youths and the generations that will come after them on whose shoulders the responsibility of salvaging Africa lies. I hope that it will in some way be useful to them in their noble endeavor.

I am convinced that despite all the enormous odds, Africa still has a chance to redeem itself, not as a matter of providence, but as a result of a collective conscious effort. In the words of Epicurus, we have, as a matter of moral and historical responsibility to "concern ourselves with the healing our own lives".

Abimbola Lagunju.

Acknowledgements

My gratitude to the following:

Abiola, Afolabi and Anjola, their friends and contemporaries for being the beacon of hope of a better Africa.

Amelia Lagunju, the young matriarch, for an exemplary level of consciousness of the mission of our generation.

Caroline Ennis for her constant support and her tirelessness in discussing the points of views expressed in the book and also for proofreading the manuscript.

Abdoulaye Mbaye for the interesting discussions on *Les problemes de l'Afrique.*

Joseph Ndiaye, the curator of the *"Maison des Esclaves"* Goree Island, Senegal for his frankness and honesty in highlighting the collaboration of some Africans in Trans-Atlantic slavery.

Theo Yomi Fakayode for being a faithful and decent friend.

Abimbola Lagunju.
Dakar, Senegal, 20 January 2005.

"We must interrogate the past, the present…. and ourselves and design a route from liberation to transformation"

Cedric Mayson—Morals for Africa?

If my hands were tied with the most obstinate roots,
I would struggle to de-fiber the cord,
I would twist and turn the sinews of bloodless hands,
keeping them alive with the power of hope of freedom,
when they shall be free to take clay
from nearby streams or distant rivers
and mould their destiny, my destiny......

(From the poem "Neocolonialism" by the same author)

Where I Stand

It is another asthmatic harmattan morning.

I again lay displayed in years of history, among wares of paper, two-dimensional *griots* of my life, antiques of moths aged in casks of hands of local and foreign historians, "head"masters and relatives, moneylenders and borrowers, slaves and masters, veterans of premature cycle of nature of juvenile harvests and untimely deaths.

I look at the first piece of my exhibition, a testimony of momentary uterine arrest of time, captured by the lens of community mind in colonial existential calligraphic engineering, a temporary plus among many minuses, a priceless monistic *de Stijl* on canvass of no other reference but my geometric self. A numberless Mona abstract of *orisa*[1] connected to earth and its capricious elemental gods by crooked lines. Miles of time drawn in sands of resignation to wheels of whims of ancestral deities painted in ceremonial oil, forewater and blood and dressed in dances.

I remain the only visitor to the cemetery of my long buried days, my piles of blond shrouds in naphthalene mausoleum, tanned in the sun of unknowing eyes and curious fingers. The only living dead of first November of three hundred and sixty five feasts of all souls.

---

1. A blanket Yoruba name for gods and goddesses

I would have caressed my first monogrammed shroud, osmosing myself into its folds, had its innocence not been contaminated by the ubiquitous *head-counters* turned hunters. Drunk on their deities, they captured and bartered virtue for bondage.

The agents and their masters have this time gone, high on virgin sweat and tears. Their wake of scars demarcate the borders between the living, yet to be visited when time again purges the uterus, the dead taken captive in the orgy of their vocation and the living dead bound in fetters of sorrow.

Disembodied in mental clouds of day-less nights, life and death, thesis and antithesis, the projection on necromantic walls of what remains of me, synthesis? archimime of myself? crowds out any *ratio*, strangling disfigured remnant bits of sanity, and moulding obvious pleasures in clay of pains.

Between the first and third shrouds lies the invisible second, marked in red circles of struggles, rectangles of unwashed knuckles, buried deep in crevices between grey and white *unmatter*, *boite de memoire* of unholy transaction, the boundary between *being* and *unbeing*. This is the obituary of the living, a verdict of guilt on innocence etched with crude implements on un-passing sheet of time. A life sentence of the soul behind the bars of an inert body. There, in the confinements of its recesses, hopping among islets of its devil's archipelago, it furls and unfurls in the storms of humiliation, hunger and despair.

The *unbeing* recreates the *being*, grafts flaps of wish on absent flesh, re-resurrecting itself in stories from looms of dreams, woven in threads of barter with greedy *gods*: a reversal of the flow of river of adrenaline of fear that irrigates bondage in turn for endorphins of courage.

I do the catwalk with ancestral valiance…..

Looks clap condescending applauds as sparsely dressed summer of politeness gets stranded in harsh winter of *real politik*; walls converge in grappling hands of concrete, *unbeing* becomes hostage of panic. Cackling claustrophobia revolves in modern white stroboscopes of old pains and chains, re-echoing in the confines of scarred recesses.
Noooooooooooo! A dream call……but scream, exhausted from conflicts with dead ears, rises in diminuendo from narcoleptic exile of unconditional surrender of its instinct to conditional reflexes. It becomes a *paganised* missionary, object converted into subject of sacrilegious sainthood.

The remnants of the *being* struggle for control, grab the bull by the snout and unleash the tongue.

Of Survival and Quality

The history and the present state of contemporary Africa and the apparent quagmire that Sub-Sahara Africa has found itself in, in terms of political and social orientation, development and its rightful dignified place among the comity of nations confound the observer and present a challenge to those who honestly believe in the potentials of its un-harnessed unified capacity to improve the conditions of lives of its people and to contribute to world development.

Despite its historical claims to being the birthplace of the human race, Africa in the twenty-first century is still confined to and kept at basic survival levels more than five million years after the first African added reason and logic to instinct. Why is Africa still grappling with survival, when others on the same planet, having taken this level for given are focusing and working untiringly on improving the quality of their existence? Where does the problem lie? Who is to blame?

It is no secret that the apparently simple task of ensuring basic survival is a daunting task, a near impossibility; natural and mostly man-induced disasters appear to have conspired to limit the survival chances of the African to pre-historic times levels. Any talk of improvement of quality of life in contemporary Africa seems superfluous when mere survival continues to remain at stake.

The primary duty of the collective, under any pretext connoting an organized entity lies in enhancing the chances of its own survival by drawing on the collective effort and resources to provide conducive environment for individual survival. Survival thus becomes a crucial social responsibility of the collective towards individual members. In this situation, the individual, unhampered by inconsequential trivialities of life, feels free to harness his creative resources towards improving the quality of his existence and by extension, the quality of existence of the collective.

In Africa, it appears that the reverse is the case. The struggle for survival appears to have been left on the shoulders of the common man in an environment that does not only limit possibilities, but is also inherently hostile to potentials. The role of the state becomes an ethereal mystery only decipherable by *god-politicians* while the existence of government in its present form actively counteracts and subjugates the aspirations of the common man. This noxious cloud that hangs over the most basic needs of the African reduces any discussion (by African politicians and their foreign masters) of improvement of quality of life to a puerile daydream in a self-deluding trance of nebulous political discourse.

The question of an African contribution to world development on equal platform with other nations, not as individuals in the service of different institutions of the world or as unconnected independent individuals, becomes distant particles of a dream unintelligible to the visionary eyes of the most politically progressive of telescopes. Africa has to move unaided from basic survival stages in order to give any relevance to its intention of contribution to world development.

It does not suffice to romanticize the role of individual Africans who have excelled in different aspects of human endeavor or the forced, despicable contribution of slavery to the industrial revolution in Europe and North America as African contribution to world development. It is the unified contribution of Africa as a continent of diverse peoples and resources, making a mark predicated on its experience, its context and in its own manner, as per universally acceptable parameters that would liberate Black Africa from prejudices. That Africa has what it takes in terms of its abundant human and natural resources, the bedrocks of any cultural, industrial and technological revolution, is not in doubt even in the mind of the most cynical critic. Africa is not however known in the world to have harnessed any of these resources to the betterment of the conditions of its citizens and the world at large, rather it is known as a compliant profligate source of its human and natural resources.

Africa as a continent has lived by the principle of a *"good native"* who turns out his household and puts all his family possessions at the disposal of the foreigner in the name of hospitality, expecting to get his reward either in heaven or be recompensed with the same generosity by the beneficiary of his profligacy. The African soon faces immense odds and conditions for the smallest of concessions when his beneficiary plays host and is humbled into gratefully accepting a fraction of what he had parted with.

The ease with which Africa parts willfully with its resources or is manipulated into doing so informs the view and the behavior of others towards African resources. African resources have taken the hue of god-given *gifts*, which should either not be paid for or underpaid for. From cotton prices to African footballers' fees in Europe, the underlying concept has been the same since the first contact of the African with the foreigner. These *gifts*, either offered willingly by the African, or spiraled away under manipulation or in some cases by bullying have informed the nature of the relationship of foreigners with Africans. Unlike the African, foreigners recognize the importance of the enormous human and natural resources available in Africa as crucial in their march away from survival level to quality level. Winston Churchill, former prime minister of the United Kingdom, lent credence to this view when he said "the safety of the North and its industries is contingent on how it is able to control or manipulate the raw material base which is in…Africa particularly"[1]. It is not difficult for the common man to understand the logic behind WTOisms and trade barriers.

The continent, still unsure of the potentials of these resources and not having any social, technical or even political infrastructure in place to put them to use, took the easy route of asking the beneficiaries of its profligacy for all forms of assistance. Assistance in finished products and fractions of GDP, not means of putting their resources to use. As a chosen or imposed policy Africa seems to have sentenced itself to a beggar status, an inveterate recipient of aid, with all attending contempt. Aid to Africa is then conditioned by Africa's beneficiaries who have now metamorphosed into *donors* and development experts on a whole bundle of conditions, which benefit them on the long run and undercut Africa's chances of emerging from its vicious quagmire. The direct consequence of this is a near irreversible damage to the psyche and dignity of the African. Yoweri Museveni, Ugandan president, at the African Union Conference titled "Africa in the 21st Century: Integration and Renaissance", held in Dakar in October 2004 confessed that "aid has failed to transform Africa. Whatever aid Africa received since independence has been wiped out several times over by the losses we have suffered in trade. The greatest subversion to Africa's development has been…the protectionism in EU, Canada, USA and Japan". One is inclined to ask from the point of view of a common man and at the risk of unleashing the fury of pundits, both local and international that if the words of Mr. Museveni were true, why then do African leaders continue to accept solicited and unsolicited aid being conscious of its nefarious effects on Africa? Why have they actively participated in making aid a major industry in Africa? Why have they consciously allowed aid to transform into potent instruments of manipulation as was the case with mirrors, guns, trinkets and alcoholic drinks during the slavery period? African history appears to be going round in circles. The age-old vulnerability of the trusting African is still the same, only the price with which he sells changes with times.

The acceptance of aid and unsolicited concessions in the "forgiveness of debts" has only introduced a new dimension into the perception of Africa's resources. The donors of aid now impose their legitimate rights to these resources and even dictate the terms and conditions under which these *gifts* should reach them. There is no doubt that the historical largesse or profligacy of Africans has not brought any advantage to Africa.

The failure of African socio-economic experiment of profligacy in the name of *hospitality*, whether willingly or under duress demands that Africa should make a calculated and conscious effort to reduce the squandering of its human and natural resources and harness them to improve not only the conditions of its people but also make unquestionable technological contribution to humanity at large. Alpha Oumar Konare, the Chairman of the Commission of the Africa Union in a speech said "the requisite conditions necessary for Africa to become a force to be reckoned with, a force we can rely upon include....the optimal use of all our assets, namely the immense human and natural resources...". This is a re-echo of the preambles of the Organization of African Unity Charter that states "Conscious of our responsibility to harness the natural and human resources of our continent for the total advancement of our peoples in all spheres of human endeavor"[2] These are the echoes of the mind of any black African, but then the question of how far the African leaders are prepared to go in order to begin this process promised in 1963 and revisited in 2003 by Mr. Konare immediately comes to mind. It is not difficult to see that the answer may be *"Not too far"*, given their *"historical ties"*, and of course the fear of losing their jobs in case they step on the wrong toe of the *international community* of beneficiaries of Africa's largesse.

Some Western scholars and indeed some Africans would argue that Africa is making some progress according to its own calendar, making its own mark in its own way. This view is not only condescending but smacks of a deliberate conspiracy to delude the African that despite being stuck at survival levels of humanity's pedestal he is making some imaginary progress. The quality of life cannot be relative; therefore human endeavor to improve the quality of life cannot be condemned to "African calendar" or to some other calendar. That Africa has to quickly move up from survival level is a historical obligation that cannot be spread over some spurious calendar. Africa has to know when to call its losses (not that it has much to lose now anyway), accept past mistakes and re-organize itself as articulated by Mr. Konare so as to occupy its rightful and dignified place among nations. Black Africa could only take this place among nations when it consciously makes efforts to put its human and natural resources to useful service in order to *continuously* generate home-inspired inputs not only to enhance its survival, but to improve the quality of its existence. As a continental goal, these inputs have to be proportional to the inputs of other nations, which have had a head-start that qualifies them as *"developed"*. The parameters of measurements of these inputs cannot be different from one race to the other; the parameters are universal and are the yardsticks with which groups of peoples are measured and classified as developed or primitive. The lower the inputs of a people as per universally acceptable parameters, the lower they are put on the scale of *"development"* and the more prejudice is meted out to them.

Africa belongs to the low-input group. Some have tried to console Africans by drawing parallels between contemporary Africa and the medieval times in Europe, arguing that internecine wars, corruption, disease are part of the process which Africa has to go through; *"kinder"* social analysts prefer to compare Africa with Europe or United States of 200 years ago. They argue that Africa may have to go through the experience of those on the upper part of the inputs scale, and that this is a long process which needs the support of those on top of the scale. The African experience has shown that those on the top of the scale use debts and aid as tools to kick the African off the ladder and to undermine any possibilities of Africa's meaningful contribution except as a source of cheap raw materials. Africa is therefore left with no choice but to accept adapting outputs of other cultures to its reality.

Human history has shown that prejudices can be reversed against a group of people when their level of inputs becomes significant on the world arena. On the other hand, when the inputs of a previously performing people dwindle for any reasons, the respect and regard for the people are accordingly scaled down. The process of adapting others' outputs to Africa's plethora of problems has unsurprisingly become an onerous task, given the one-size-fits-all nature of these outputs and the inability of African leaders to either out-rightly reject those outputs that are prejudicial or cause the few useful ones to be transformed by Africans into more suitable tools. Africa is consequently regarded as a continent where tested and proven ideas fail.

Africans do know that only a very small fraction of foreign-conceived solutions are useful and are not potentially harmful to the African cause. The inability of African leaders to capitalize on the few workable outputs to begin the process of transformation of the continent is what raises questions and consternation. When these questions are raised, African leaders have their standard plethora of excuses linked to others but themselves. These excuses of debt burden, wars, trade barriers, unresponsive (to their stretched arms) international community are overflogged and nebulous; they smack of lack of vision and courage to seek and provide alternative home-grown solutions. Rather than sift through the mess of solutions (aid, debts, political orientation, etc.) and find the right adaptable output and identify the right partners, African leaders ask for more *solutions* in aid and debts. Africa is further not helped by placard-carrying activists in other cultures who either put these arguments into the mouth of the African leaders or help them echo these excuses. These arguments engender an acceptance of helplessness and undermine any desire or drive to explore latent potentials.

The *"passionate intensity"*[3] of liberal activists in other cultures (who though vote the wrong way when the subject of their activism becomes a threat to their lifestyle and privileges) and shameless appeals of some African leaders to the *"conscience"* of *"international community"* to provide crumbs have succeeded in alienating from the mind of the African the conviction that Africa has the potential, can, and should make a bold mark in the course of human endeavor to improve the quality of its existence. Henry Kissinger, the former American Secretary of State declared in a book that it is only the "moral commitment of the American people and the international community"[4] that could save Africa which he described as *"the festering disaster of our age."* Mr. Tony Blair, the British Prime minister (of regime-change fame) in Davos, Switzerland and on numerous other occasions declared Africa to be a *"scar"* on the conscience of the world in need of major plastic surgery of debt relief and more aid. In order to soothe the *festering wound* or conduct a keloid-inducing plastic surgery on the *scar*, Mr. Blair's Commission for Africa Report released in March 2005 recommended that "….the developed world must increase and improve its aid……"[5].

The incessant appeals of African leaders to the *"international community"* constitute a contradiction of the romanticized *"bravery and valor"* of the African man. In many black African cultures, manliness is first and foremost defined by the ability of a man to put his house in order and to act as a responsible head of his household by providing for, and protecting his family. It is an abomination to see an African man lamenting the failures of his manliness in the market place. While people may empathize with the consequences of his failures, he has lost the right to be called a man. Western liberal ideology and restless social activism have however taught African leaders that there is a duality to manhood. It has become acceptable and fashionable in the international arena to lament failures, attributing these failures to someone else's making and playing the helpless victim; and on the other hand use whatever morsels or concessions are bestowed by the *"international community"* to exercise manliness at home, either as a puppet or as a dictator. The re-echoing of problems of Africa by political and social activists in other cultures and the deliberate and conscious portrayal of apparent helplessness of the continent have in some way institutionalized ineptitude of African governments and peoples. Firstly, it has succeeded in convincing the African peoples and their leaders that their problems are insurmountable and that others are responsible for these problems and solutions have to come from outside in the form of concessions, aid and *"development"*. Secondly, it has also taught the *"international community"* to *"concede"* to handing out morsels of aid with one hand, and with the other hand subvert any attempts by Africa (not that there are any concerted moves to do so by Africa) to liberate itself from these shackles by convincing African leaders to entrench themselves and their citizens in the ever deepening hole of debts and debt servicing. The *donors* then offer incommensurate gigantic technical support for the management of these debts and their derisive *aid*. The absurdity of this *"aid"* becomes more evident when weighed against how much capital leaves Africa in the name of debt servicing. This *"aid"* blown out of proportion by the Western media represents a fraction of unsung capital robbery committed by *"donors"* in Africa under the banner of *"debt servicing"*.

It is a natural human instinct that when confronted with immense odds, one puts all his resources to use to overcome these odds. This is also applicable to groups of peoples as nations, as a race, as ethnic or religious groups. In the case of a race or a nation, it is fundamental that internal differences be put aside and a common front be found to overcome the difficulties. Appropriate matured political philosophy, whether as a civil religion or ideology is crucial in this regard. The history of persecution of Jews around the world and the seeming un-end to these injustices culminated in the convocation of the first Zionist Congress in 1897. The Congress sought to unite the whole of Jewry in order to put an end to this persecution. Many other focused congresses and meetings with the same objective would follow this first initiative. In other words, conscious collective efforts were made by Jews as a people to overcome the odds facing them in all corners of the world. A direct or indirect consequence of these concerted efforts is the emergence of a powerful nation of Jews

(Israel) strong enough to take on any nation that dares to repeat what happened in Nazi Germany. Even if there are still occasional anti-semitic sentiments in some parts of the world, the great lengths to which the political leaders of these countries go to to denounce these sentiments and the magnitude of the state apparatus which they invest in curbing these sentiments are a confirmation of the successful strategy of Jews in affirming their right to self-esteem and dignity, not as a political concession but as a hard-earned right, supported by the might of their tiny nation.

Black African peoples, who have literally and figuratively been victims of atrocities for most of their existence, have not, not at any point of their history, been able to set aside their internal differences to overcome the odds that face them as a race. It is not enough to struggle to get the title of *"human beings"* or to veer off on some narcissistic mission of exhumations of historical heroism in order to claim a place among other races. These claims have to be backed up with a continuous conscious process of re-inventing the self to meet the challenges of the world and thereby earn dignity and respect as a result of input, not as a political or moral concession. Unfortunately, Africa is synonymous with energy-sapping and time-consuming internal divisions founded on a repertoire of legitimate and illegitimate excuses ranging from ethnic differences, through differences in imported religious to differences in official foreign languages. *Democratization* of problems rather than solution has become a hallmark of Africa. This *medusa* of problems naturally attracts ad hoc hydra-headed solutions leaving untouched the fundamental question of what makes Africa so vulnerable to self-destructive tendencies. Ad hoc solutions are by their nature very attractive to all the actors involved in a conflict or its resolution. The parties involved in the conflict, the *"problem democrats"* feel vindicated as to the *legitimacy* of their claims (some even get placated with very important government posts); those involved in resolving the conflict have a sense of achievement, their conscience appeased that they have done some good and hopefully would reap more benefits than their initial investments in seminars, hotel costs and travels. It is, in the parlance of development pundits, a *win-win situation*.

It is a failure of imagination of legitimate and illegitimate African leaders that in *"democratizing"* problems and seeking external ad hoc solutions, they have in any way advanced the course of the continent and the black race. On the contrary, they have succeeded in conveying to the world a caricature image of Africa as a continent devoid of possibilities of any inputs; and thus fuelled the fires of prejudices against all black peoples of the world.

Africa has to consciously and honestly search for the fundamental problem on which other problems which have become the trademark of Africa are founded. It is a search for the body of the medusa, its very heart. That problems exist in Africa, and have been mutating, multiplying and haunting generations of Africans is a known and accepted fact. Looking beyond the obvious problems and extricating the *fundamental* from its recesses is where the challenge lies. There cannot be any advancement if the diagnosis of the fundamental is wrong.

Africa has been an open field for multitudes of studies and social experiments directed at diagnosing the *fundamental* and proffering solution. It is an absurdity of our helplessness that others who are alien to African culture, traditions and philosophy of life come with different tools and theory to decipher African problems. It is a known fact that the *solutions* of these *"experts"* have not in any way changed the continent. On the contrary, the repertoire of ideas they have proffered and experimented appears to have further muddled up the situation.

The overrated assumption that all problems disappear under the blanket solution of Western-style development is not only a gross misunderstanding of the underlying fundamental problem but it also highlights the unwillingness of African actors and their foreign development technical advisors to address the issue. The very nature of this problem renders ineffective any imported armchair economic theory or socio-political experiments.

When Africa finally arrives, unaided, at the point of diagnosing the fundamental problem which it faces, and proposes an appropriate solution, development will come from within as a *fait accompli,* not as an import. Development will come as a collective internal drive of African peoples based on their conviction to improve the chances of their survival by improving the quality of their lives.

This mechanism to kick-start this collective internal drive cannot be imported or exported.

Humanizing by de-Africanizing.

Blacks are born blacks irrespective of where they are born or whatever nationality they may carry. The heritage of the color of their skin is primordial over all other social or political conditions of their environment. They face prejudices predicated on the color of their skin in any environment where they constitute a minority. Even here on African soil, the minority white population has by instinct arrogated a superior attitude to itself vis-à-vis its black hosts. In the mind of many people including the most liberal of other cultures, being a Black African is synonymous with all possible evils: diseases, wars, corruption, famine, drought, drugs and an infinite ineptitude to redeem himself from his precarious condition. This perception has its origins not only in the ease with which foreigners overran Africa and sentenced it to the periphery of humanity; but is also rooted in supremacist ideology and views of Western scholars, politicians and the clergy.

Georges Curvier, a French biologist, once wrote that "the African manifestly approaches the monkey tribe. The hordes of which this variety is composed have always remained in a complete state of barbarism…"[6] This position was also shared by America's Thomas Jefferson who wrote "…I advance it therefore as a suspicion only that the blacks whether originally a distinct race or made distinct by time and circumstances, are inferior to the whites in the endowments of the mind and body…"

Hendrick Verwoerd, the architect of grand apartheid said in 1953 "Natives will be taught from childhood to realize that equality with Europeans is not for them"[7]. He said further "there is no place for the black in the European community above the level of certain forms of labour". Hendrick Verwoerd deserves credit for giving credence to Malcom X's beliefs, by expressing clearly in public what others have shied away from saying but have always manifested covertly as an accepted fact of life, a societal behavior-regulatory philosophy. Britain's Lord Milner also had this to say of early South African politics: "A political equality of white and black is impossible, the white man must rule because he is elevated by many, many steps above the black man"[8]. And Frantz Fanon in his book, "Wretched of the Earth" claimed that WHO's Dr. Carothers in the nineteen fifties crowned it all by arriving at the conclusion that the black man is equivalent to a lobotomized white man[9].

Have these views changed over time or have they been closeted in the recesses of politically correct behavior?

Socio-political activism in countries with sizable black populations has in some ways suppressed overt prejudices against the black race, and politically correct racial interaction has become a kind of public signboard. While the blacks would like to think that they earned it through their long social struggle, the whites would like to think that they granted it as a matter of moral concession. A concession that is not founded on any convictions. This privilege remains relevant for as long as it does not in any way threaten their current lifestyle or their long term strategy of keeping themselves on the top of world's social scale. As Ahmed Sekou Toure, the founding president of Guinea said: "when a white man knows that a certain black man has positive worth, that he is honest, that he says what he thinks…that he is humane and just, the white man thinks nonetheless: 'Help him to develop himself? That would be to put our privileges in jeopardy'." It is no gainsaying that when privileges become threatened and social circumstances compel a review of socially or racially acceptable behavior, this concession may be withdrawn. Where would the Black African in any part of the world stand if this happened?

The roots of all black peoples of the world can be traced back to Sub-Sahara Africa; and the largest concentration of black peoples is still in Sub-Sahara Africa. This part of the African continent has an enormous moral obligation and responsibility towards all the black peoples of the world by consciously redeeming itself and establishing itself as a proud place of reference. This proud reference is still elusive and Africa is known worldwide as a failed continent, a *"festering disaster"*, *"a scar on the conscience of the world"*. African has been transformed into a source of consolation for even poorer (than Africans) peoples of other parts of the world, whose malicious politicians go to great lengths to convince them that despite the political and economic difficulties that they are confronted with, they are still better off than Africans. In the hands of politicians and in the minds of the citizens of these countries, Africa has become the barometer of measurement of poverty and woes.

The relegation of Black Africa to the back seat of humanity, in part as a deliberate strategy of others, and in a large part as a direct consequence of the ineptitude of Black Africans themselves to collectively forward their own cause and make a mark on equal footing with other peoples of the world has alienated *Africans* who have been exposed to other cultures. Many black Africans whether on African soil or in diaspora who have had some exposure to other cultures fiercely embrace them and go to great lengths to distance themselves from Black Africa. The Afrocentric School of thought contends that "human beings cannot divest themselves of culture;........They may, of course, choose to opt out of their own cultural heritage and appropriate that of some other people. This is rarely the case, however, with Europeans. They do not choose to become Indians or Chinese or Africans. In fact, the **only people** who have totally distanced themselves from their cultural origins are Africans.... They have been victimized by the negative image of Africa and have therefore concluded that they want nothing to do with Africa."[10]

Even here on the African soil, black Africans who have close dealings with Berbers, Bedouins, Moors and Arabs in a master-slave relationship are always quick to point out that they are not Africans but members of any of these tribes. Seizing on this lamentable state of mind, and needing to show the world that they are on some other rung of humanity different from that of black Africans, North Africans refer to sub-Saharan Africans as "*Africans*", meaning black with all attending ills they associate with this identity. The relationship between North Africans and Black Africans has never been a relationship of mutual respect and equality despite the rhetoric of African leaders. Black Africans who have had cause to visit any of the North African countries have experienced overt and covert prejudice of the citizens and authorities of these countries. This prejudice is not premised on the legitimacy or not of being there; it is squarely premised on the color of the skin. A female BBC African service journalist on vacation in one of these North African countries in 2003 reported her unpalatable experience because of the color of her skin. The state of Black Africans living in these countries is lamentable. In some of these countries, black Africans are relegated to slave status and in some other countries where they seek to express themselves, they are systematically eliminated as is the case in Darfour in Western Sudan in 2003, 2004 and 2005, where according to a UN report "the government and Arab militias forces are launching a racial cleansing campaign against non-Arab tribes in Darfour area to the west of Sudan".

The lighter-skinned Africans particularly in the Horn of Africa whenever the opportunity arises also seek to distance themselves from the black race. An acquaintance, a Minister from an African country was invited to a conference in one of these countries; the Minister during some free period decided to go into town without the paraphernalia of her office provided by the conference. She wanted to get to meet the people of the country and chat. Her first experience was with a woman-beggar in the street on whom she took pity and offered her the equivalent of ten dollars. The beggar was torn between the amount offered her and her *dignity*! The money eventually won the day; the beggar took the money from the minister and offered a prayer that God should forgive her for taking money from the poor black woman! This happened in 2002. The headquarters of the African Union as was that of the Organization of African Unity is based in Addis Ababa, Ethiopia. Numerous press reports have reported the problems which black diplomats working in the headquarters of this body and other African secretariats based in this country face. But hear Emperor Haile Selassie on the arguments for creation of Organization of African Unity: "But through all that has been said and written and done in these years, there runs

a common theme. Unity is the accepted goal. We argue about tech-
niques and tactics. But when semantics are stripped away, there is
little argument among us. We are determined to create a union of
Africans". One is inclined to think that either the late Emperor was
expressing a personal dream that was not in any way connected to
the dream of his people or he was speaking on behalf of his people
who have gradually moved away from this lofty idea. The glaring
reality today is a contradiction of this vision; a divisive spectrogram
where the black African is accorded the lowest band on the spectrum of the so called African unity.

It is a tragedy of black Africa that members of this race either of
lighter skin or exposed to other cultures seek to distance themselves
from being identified with the black race

Like most minority groups in the world, Blacks living outside the
African continent are victims of prejudice predicated on their color.
Their color activates the danger signal in the minds of their *hosts*
particularly in areas where it is an unwritten but known law that "*no
blacks allowed in the grounds*". Under the guise of political correctness in Western countries, this intrusion is not overtly challenged
but covertly despised. The local police elevate their warning signals
to high alert. This is a scenario which all blacks living in Western
countries have accustomed themselves to; some ignoring it, some
challenging it, most avoiding it. This is a scenario that constantly
challenges the dignity of a black African.

In Asian and Middle East countries with no *"politically correct"*
racial policies, the Black African is treated with open contempt and
the most law-abiding behavior could be criminalized on the whims
of the authorities. The black man remains an anathema in these
countries. Moreover, it is a paradox of hospitality that China, India

and Pakistan, whose citizens could be found in all corners of the world, and with quite a large number of their citizens living in Africa are particularly hostile to Black Africans who have for one reason or the other found themselves in their part of the world. A common denominator to all these countries is that as a rule, dignity is denied the Black African simply because of his color. The fate of Africans taken away into slavery in Asia is still a mystery till this day.

Among many other things, the Black African in the twenty-first century is still compelled to add the demand of dignity to his list of daily struggles.

If all the rights of perception of black Africans and the way others relate with them whether ill-informed or not were to be conceded on the grounds of territorial ownership, then it is a moral duty for the African to have a critical look at foreigners' perception and the way they relate to the African on African soil.

There are three main categories of foreigners, born in Africa or immigrants alike, living in Africa. The first category is exclusive to Europeans and other Westerners. The other two categories are applicable to Europeans and other Westerners, Asians and Arabs alike.

The first category, exclusively Europeans, could be described as obdurate guardians of colonial mentality and culture. Their view of the African has not changed even with political independence of African states. They believe that Africans and its resources were created for their use and should thus be exploited with impunity for their material comfort. They keep to themselves, keeping their contact with the African to the barest minimum through their servants. They still keep their tea parties, derbies and they go to great lengths to keep the African away from their colonial *heritage*. These are the open or closeted apologists of the *"Immorality Act"*. They serve as the source of all derogatory information on the African and his irredeemability. They serve as the *local international community*, *experts* on Africa, whose views and opinions become critical for the foreign international community in their decisions on the government in power. This group sees nothing good in Africa. While they have the choice to leave for their home countries which they make ready allusions to when condemning Africa, they choose to remain in Africa and act as tin gods, with African servants to attend to them. They flaunt their contribution to the local economy as their *raison d'être*. They are the ubiquitous hosts to other Westerners who have come to Africa for short stays either to work or on vacation. Through their solicited or unsolicited *in-country training* programs for these new-comers, they get to convince even the most liberal of placard-carrying activist of the precariousness of the African cause and his imminent abysmal destiny. Under this obnoxious tutelage the latter, even if they had come to Africa with an open heart would acquire a superior and condescending attitude towards the African. There is no doubt that this group of foreigners in itself constitutes not only a clog in the wheels of progress of Africa, but it also reaches out to poison the minds of those from other cultures who otherwise mean well for the cause of the continent.

The second category is constituted by economic mercenaries. They are just in Africa to make money. This group goes to great lengths to have friends in important places. They move with the elite. They despise the common people and only have exploitative contacts with them. They have no loyalty to their host country and their interest is solely based on returns on their investments. They see all Africans, irrespective of their social status as tools to use to achieve their objectives. Some serve as the ubiquitous middlemen and women with contacts everywhere. Some members of this group act as economic advisors to African kleptocrats; they know where to purchase guns in case of conflicts and they serve as conduits for stolen wealth among many other activities. They have in no small measure contributed to the conflicts and the poor state of the economy of Africa. This group acting either directly or in tandem with the ubiquitous multinationals has immensely contributed to the importation, implantation and institutionalization of the alien concept of corruption in Africa.

A common feature of these two groups is that they have little or no regard for their hosts. They see their hosts as tools and means to attain their short or long term objectives.

Members of the third category are at the other extreme of the spectrum of the first two. They do not see themselves as descendants of another race on another soil. They are true to their environment; and have little or no attachments to their native countries. They share the pains of Black history, live the consequences in the present and share the hope of the common African man for a good future. They work hard like all conscientious black Africans to contribute their quota to their society. They are more African than black Africans as the saying goes. They unfortunately constitute a small minority among foreigners on African soil.

Alien Form of Governance—Our Curse

Most African countries attained their independence either through armed struggles or dialogue in the sixties. The politically independent Africa was born into an ideologically polarized world and the pre-independence vision of fathers of modern Africa leaders of a strong unified Africa by and large became a casualty of the cold war. It served the interests of the two ideological blocks to see Africa divided and polarized along their own philosophy of life. Though the two blocks had strong differences in their political and social structures based on capitalist and socialist ideologies, they both had a common goal as regards Africa; that Africa should never constitute a threat either militarily or economically to their interests. This, they could only achieve if Africa was in disarray. It is tempting to imagine what would have been the relationship between the two blocks as regards Africa in a hypothetical event of an economically strong and militarily capable and unified Africa during this period. This however was not to be; and Africa became a free and willing field for putting their military and espionage theoretical lessons into practice.

From abroad, dividing lights have been beamed on ethnic differences and imbalances in power and resource sharing among ethnic groups in different countries in Africa. As recently as February 2005, the Belgian government made available to journalists accompanying the Belgian foreign minister on a trip to war-torn Democratic Republic of Congo (held together by fragile peace), a DRC-Country profile document in which the CVs of the members of the Congolese government were included. It was alleged in this Belgian government write-up that the president of the DRC, Joseph Kabila and one his vice presidents were of foreign origin. The content of this document later became public knowledge in DRC. The inherent intention of this document was clear, but given the past experience of the war-fatigued Congolese people with the Belgians, the document and its authors were treated with the contempt which they deserved.

In post-independence Africa however, the altruism of foreigners was taken as sacrosanct; Africans naively believed in these foreign-engineered ethnic imbalances and fought each other to correct it. It is a known fact that until the arrival of Europeans, Tutsis and Hutus in Burundi and Rwanda were known to have lived in peace and harmony with each other for centuries under their own arrangements. This arrangement was however disrupted and centuries-old harmony, under a foreign-engineered arrangement, transformed into cycles of massacres of genocidal magnitudes.

Having beamed light on all possible differences and imbalances among African peoples, foreigners convinced African leaders of the appropriateness of their ideological tools to correct these imbalances, and, true to its avidity for self-destructive tendencies, Africa fiercely embraced their newly found knowledge and ideology. Some made camp with capitalists, others with communists and yet some became bedmates of apartheid. A new lucrative vocation of military advisers was created by the engineers of confusion in order to keep the fire of hatred and differences burning. Thus, foreigners provided the cause, the ideology, the strategy and the weapons and Africans provided the victims.

The founding fathers of Africa and indeed the latter day African leaders, obsessed with keeping themselves in power and naively trusting the altruism of the foreign camp on which side they stood, failed to see that they were victims as much as those that they were killing and destroying. As it was during the slavery and colonial times, the natural self-preservation instinct and unity among black Africans was allowed to be undermined. Africa was, and continues to be susceptible and vulnerable to foreign manipulations.

The different ideological and philosophical approaches to gover-nance in post independence Africa failed to address the cause of our vulnerability from an African perspective and to clearly diagnose the problem before proposing solutions. Amilcar Cabral conceded that "History teaches us that certain circumstances make it very easy for foreign people to impose their dominion..........." What were these circumstances?

The approaches adopted in the diagnosis of these circumstances and solution proffered had their shortcomings in being offshoots or negations of different European schools of thought. Either they swung towards socialism as an antidote to the capitalist colonial sys-tem or they further entrenched the colonial system of governance. More importantly was that they all had their basis in what they claimed to have mentally rejected with the attainment of political *independence*. This so-called *independence* comes under question when viewed in the light of Dr. Chancellor James Williams' declara-tion that "those who do become **free** in fact, will no longer grab the white man's ideologies....whether capitalism, Western version of democracy or communism, without a critical review and analysis to determine whether Africa's own traditional system, when updated, may not be superior and best fitted to meet the aspirations of the Black world.".

General Charles de Gaulle of France, afraid of a leftist swing of its former colonies and a possible consequent compromise of French interests in its colonies, canvassed in the Guinean parliament for the conservation of French culture and doctrines which "have been able to contribute to revealing the quality of men.." by warning that "there will always be ideologies like a screen, like a flag to go before it; it would not be the first time in history of the world that ethnic and national interests march behind signs"[11]. He needn't have worried so much. A common feature of immediate post-*independence,* and indeed present day Africa is the conservation of colonial form of public administration with all its methods of repression and tools of manipulation. The *"reconverting"* of the system which Sekou Toure talked of, if it happened at all, was short-lived either willingly or under external pressure. Post-independence African systems of governance sought and found its only reference in the colonial methods of administration. Agostinho Neto, the first president of Angola, confirmed this by declaring that "we do not find a single country in Africa which does not maintain preferential relations with its former metropole, even through the absorption of the inevitable cultural values of a regime of a colonial type. What is more, the forms of exploitation do not end......"[12] The system of governance, the judiciary and the parliament were fashioned after one colonial form or the other. It is an absurdity of Africa that the judiciary and educational system of many African countries still strongly retain their colonial roots. In the case of the judiciary, there are the *orthodox* courts and native (sometimes called traditional or customary) courts. One is inclined to ask who is the native in 21st century self-governed Africa? Is there something wrong in merging the so-called orthodox judiciary with traditional one to produce something more understandable and readily accessible to the largely traditional African population? It is an absurdity that Westernized Africans and their international managers in 2004 and 2005 expressed worries of miscarriage of justice in village courts set up by the Rwandan government to try genocide suspects! The performance of these courts has proved the inherent superiority of unexplored home-grown African ideas to imported ones.

If there have been cases of miscarriage of justice perpetrated in Africa, (and there have been many) these have always been associated with the orthodox courts and not the traditional ones where everyone has a say without bogus protocol.

The colonial administrative system was created by the colonialists to facilitate the oppression of the colonized peoples and to repress any form of challenge to their pillage and enslavement. The administrative structures were not put in place to favor the oppressed but to serve the oppressors. With the attainment of independence, one would have expected that this form of governance and public administration would be gradually dismantled and substituted with an alternative home-grown, people-friendly system of governance that would plug all the holes of plunder committed by the colonialists. The famous declaration of Sekou Toure that the colonial "structures that we have inherited would be reconverted so that they would serve the aspirations of the people" was however not to be. The system that facilitated the plundering of Africa by the colonialists was adopted by African leaders to further plunder the continent. In the words of Frantz Fanon, "spoilt children of yesterday's colonialism and of today's national governments organize the loot of whatever national resources exist"[13].

The erstwhile plunderers still smarting from what they lost on granting political independence now shout foul on their African successors. The founders of corruption and plunder now call their pupils names. In order to reverse the situation and armed with incredible foresight, the former colonialists invented institutions which would slowly permeate into the very structure of the *"independent"* national governments. The system of governance and public administration structures in present day Africa gradually evolved from a colonial tool into a powerful field of play for the IMF and the World Bank. In present day Africa, ministries bear similar names across the continent on the prescription of the IMF and the World Bank. The functions are required to be similar in order to facilitate the parasitic work of the pundits of these neo-colonialist institutions. Regrettably, Africa has not deemed it fit to put its feet down and insist on home grown alternatives that would serve its people.

Some would be quick to argue that there would be less misery if these institutions were to function properly. This is an illusion. The alien nature of these structures and the legacy of pillage and plunder which they represent make it impossible to expect any useful outputs from them.

As a deliberate long-term destabilizing strategy, the colonialists invented ethnic imbalance in their administrative structure. They engineered the domination of one ethnic group over the other in their administration and laid grounds for future political discord between the *"privileged"* ethnic group and others. Docility and amenability, not merits, were the criteria of selection of the favorite ethnic group. The *"privileged"* ethnic group with its strong presence in the colonial public administration system came to regard itself as *"god-ordained"* ruling tribe or group in the post-independence period. Attempts to correct these historical anomalies have been reasons for war in some African countries; in others the less privileged ethnic group engages in deliberate derailment of the system. In countries where this anomaly has not resulted in wars, and consensus on a more ethnically representative system has been reached, public administration has had to face the problem of having an incompetent and ill-motivated workforce. All these factors have gradually led to a systemic dysfunction of the administrative system.

In the absence of any viable African alternative to governance and public administration, the African successors of the colonialists dearly held on to their heritage of colonial system. The common man whose aspirations during the liberation struggle had been based on the emergence of a new system, where he would not just be a number, but an active member soon became disillusioned. This appears logical given that the system was in the first instance created by the colonialists to serve their own interests to the complete exclusion of the interests of their African victim. The common man, not understanding the absurdity of keeping this oppressive colonial system and its tools of oppression intact in the post-independence period soon became disoriented and consequently estranged and disconnected from the system of public administration and governance. The administrative structure with its accompanying political system came to acquire an abstract form in his mind, and he began to feel anonymous in the *new dispensation*.

The abstract form of this alien form of governance and the complete disconnection of the common man from it inform the relegation of any imported form of *modern* governance to the backseat in favor of a more familiar, home-grown traditional one in which "the individual is very much exposed to the community and anonymity is virtually out of the question"[14] as John Mbiti declared in his paper titled *General Manifestation of African Religiosity.*

Western democracy falls within this alien form of modern governance and does not and will not have an appropriate response to the aspirations of the common African man because the alien nature, manipulation, oppression and exploitation inherent in the historical *raison d'être* of the system have alienated any form of possible association or even the remotest sense of ownership of this system from his mind.

The Response of the Common Man

The feeling of anonymity of the African common man within the abstract structure of governance and public administration left by the colonialists and adopted by African leaders engenders his potential disregard for system-imposed civic duties or norms. He *deregulates* his behavior as a form of silent protest against the system and as a means of survival in an unfamiliar environment. In the words of Wole Soyinka, "abstract...fetters...make passionate revolutionaries of the most cosseted life"[15]. The defacement of major African cities, crime, and systematic destruction of scarce public infrastructures are all symptoms of estrangement of the common man with the system of governance. There cannot be a sense of ownership of an abstract alien system and its structures.

It goes without saying that the same African would behave quite differently in his own village or community where he readily identifies with the traditional community form of governance. He lives within the norms of his environment, respects the tradition and culture even when he is convinced that these might be based on superstitions. In the same manner, he would behave differently in other cultures. Most black African professionals who have left Africa to work in Western countries are known to be very hardworking, assiduous and competent. This attitude sometimes surprises their Western colleagues who are inclined to think that if Africa has such hard working and competent professionals, why is it that the continent continues to face the enormous problems which it faces.

The black African working in this environment does not necessarily form any opinion on the abstract form or otherwise of the system in which he works, nor does he worry about anonymity or not within it. He is simply part of a system that works for its creators. And he has other concerns too. He feels constantly challenged to prove his ability to his colleagues; and he contents himself by doing much more than is expected of him. Contrary to what people like to think, financial remunerations, though important occupy a secondary place in his mind.

The African professionals working in Africa are not less competent than those working abroad. Their presence is however unfelt because they fall into the African society mentality trap; the team becomes abstract and they function as independent individuals within this intangible nebula.

The new era of pseudo-democracy in Africa provides a thriving environment for further entrenchment of *deregulated* behavior and its consequent social ills. The ruling party irrespective of how it gets to be the ruling party wants to stay in the good books of the electorate, not by doing *good* for the society, but by allowing the electorate to do, in the name of *civil liberties* what it chooses within the framework of *deregulated* behavior. The ruling party employs a deliberate confusion of civil liberties with civic norms as a strategy. This strategy is useful both on the home front and the international arena. On the home front, it serves to obfuscate the common man's potential demand by revolt for a favorable and decent environment for the legitimate pursuit of means of survival. In the international arena, it serves to convince the international *community* of the ruling party's commitment to *"human rights"*. Under this smokescreen, the ruling party puts his colonial inheritance of instruments and structures of plunder into use.

Like the common man on the street, the civil service workers perceive the civil service as an enormous and abstract system, the role of which is questionable in their minds vis-à-vis their concept of a society. They adopt an indifferent attitude to their work. It is common knowledge that the civil service system is Africa is fraught with ineptitude and disorganization. Many cases have been reported in Africa where occasionally, the government in power makes a show of attempting to put the civil service *"on track"* by actively tracking punctuality of civil service workers at their posts. The show goes on for a week or two and soon everyone tires of the game and returns to business of lackadaisicality as usual.

The public office holder also sees the public service as an abstract structure towards which he feels no responsibility or sense of being there to serve. Like his common man compatriot, he feels also anonymous and estranged within this abstract situation and at a higher level shows complete disregard not only for the responsibilities conferred on him by his position but also on the direct consequences of his attitude. Under this situation, he gives no second thought to diverting into his pocket, funds which are meant to deliver public goods and services. He sees no link between his action and children dying from preventable diseases, the decaying infrastructure and the squalor that surrounds him in his opulence.

Behavior *deregulation* eventually leads to the known African trademarks of social disorder, corruption, wars, ineffective public services, non-functional public utilities. These problems of attitude later result in dire economic situations, that lead African leaders to

Bretton Woods institutions, who in their *"wisdom"* and *"knowledge of Africa"* interpret the situation as an economic one and prescribe among other things further *deregulations* which translate into more social disorder.

Rudolf Julius Emmanuel, a German physicist, described entropy in his second law of Thermodynamics as a tendency of natural processes to move from order to disorder. In the case of Africa, this process was actively assisted by the incursion of foreigners on African soil and the subsequent occupation of the lands and minds of the people. It is an unfortunate course of African history that post-independence Africa still continues along this process. This same law also states that the greater the entropy in a given system, the less the available energy for useful work. Increasing entropy has consumed useful energy that could bring about any meaningful development of Africa inspired by Africans despite enormous human and natural resources in the continent.

One may ask the question that if the black African were indifferent to and felt anonymous within the imposed system, why then would Africans engage each other in wars which at times are senseless in order to take control of this same system? It would appear logical that there should be a general unwillingness to spill blood over an abstract concept.

It is generally assumed, based on alien economic theories, that most wars in Africa can be linked to access to and control of resources. This is true for the engineers of these rebellions, who in most cases are foreign interests and their local agents. The common man, the foot soldier in these wars does not engage in these conflicts for this reason. According to Wole Soyinka, the common man represents "...a people misled into making sacrifices for..... the entrenchment

of an exploitative socio-economic mutuality"[16]. He sees his participation in these conflicts as a probable means of substituting the
abstract system in which he has been reduced to an anonymous status with a more concrete system in which he will have a tangible and
recognizable role to play. If the side on which he has fought wins, he
soon becomes disillusioned in the post-war period when the abstract
concept which he fought to do away with reinvents itself. If his side
of the conflict loses, he remains with the thoughts and hopes of
overturning the tables one day. In both cases, he remains a latent
tool to be manipulated at any time into another conflict with the
promise of his desired change.

It is always assumed that all Africans who migrate out of Africa have
either done so under the pretext of economic or political reasons.
This assumption is not entirely correct. There is a large unsung
number of Africans who choose to leave Africa not for those two
reasons but to escape the hopelessness of chaos that reigns in Africa.
Faced with enormous and apparently insurmountable odds, they
choose to escape from the anarchy of their environment, the lack of
vision of their leaders and from the absence of serious political will
to address the problems facing the African continent. They look for
some semblance of sanity in a potentially hostile environment,
where they are often obliged to overlook in W.E.B du Bois' words,
"personal disrespect and mockery……. ridicule and systematic
humiliation"[17] because they stand on the other side of the color line.

The obsession of some Africans to desperately escape the problems
of Africa for menial and humiliating jobs in Western countries
should be a cause of concern for African leaders who understand
what their role is supposed to be. It is claimed that more than
60'000 African professionals leave African shores every year. The
shame of standing on long queues to obtain visas and the humilia-

tion meted out to Africans in Western embassies should be a source of concern to responsible governments. They could as a minimum insist on a dignified treatment of their citizens applying for visas; unfortunately, these governments watch as their citizens, which the society has enormously invested in training, are humiliated just to obtain visas to go and enslave themselves in Western countries. It is common knowledge that skilled Africans (doctors, lawyers, engineers) offer themselves for humiliating jobs in Western countries. Dignity becomes a price they have to pay on their own soil and in a foreign land for the lack of vision and the ineptitude of the leaders of their homelands.

At home or abroad, for the past 600 years, the fate of the black African has been the sacrifice of his dignity, his hopes and aspirations, his life.

The Nature of Evil

"The sad truth is that most evil is done by people who never make up their minds to be either good or bad".

—*Hannah Arendt, Thinking (The life of the Mind, 1978)*

Most natural phenomena embody opposing concepts in clear terms. In some cases however, this duality is not clearly apparent and the existence of one takes form in the negation of the other. Between opposing concepts are areas which are referred to as grey, which implies that a natural phenomenon may be a continuum of concepts from one extreme to the opposing extreme. That light is the opposing extreme of darkness is an accepted fact; the variations in the intensity of light between the morning and night constitute the continuum of grey areas or *relative-ness* of these two opposing concepts.

In the course of human and societal development, opposing concepts of good and evil have evolved to protect humanity and societies from anarchy and chaos. Unlike natural phenomena, these concepts tend to be absolute and universal with very little or no grey areas between the two extremes. These concepts find expression in form of values and ethics. Societies have evolved appropriate mechanisms either in form of a written law or unwritten code of conduct to safeguard the sanctity of these ethics and values. This would appear logical. Good or evil cannot be relative as Sophists argued and their modern day apologists like to echo.

Some may argue that cultural and traditional contexts are important determinants in the applicability of these universal concepts. This is true, but this does not imply a change in the nature of the concepts. A universally accepted good cannot undergo cultural transformations into evil and vice versa. Human life for example cannot be more precious in one culture and valueless in another. Life is life. The violation of its sacredness cannot be relative. Sometimes, an *apparent* good act may be used as a smokescreen for evil intentions. The transitory good derived from this situation does not in any way change the evil nature of the whole act. The combination of good-evil is evil. An intentional evil act that under some serendipitous events turns out to have good results cannot by virtue of these results negate its evil nature. It still remains evil.

Interests have a special impact on the perception and therefore applicability of these universal concepts. In the name of interests, the concept of good and evil loses its oppositionality, its components become fused into one lopsided sophistic doctrine of *"what is good for us"* or *"what benefits us"*, with total disregard for the evil consequences of this position on the other party. In such situations, the party with interests, recognizing the evil consequences of their actions on the other party, goes to great lengths to justify the "morality" of their actions. Jules Ferry (1832–1893), the Prime Minister of France, from [1880–1881, 1883–1885] in his speech for justifying colonial expansion said "Gentlemen, we must speak more loudly and more honestly! We must say openly that indeed the higher races have a right over the lower races….I repeat, that the superior races have a right because they have a duty. They have the duty to civilize the inferior races…." Mr. Jules Ferry attempted to justify the consequences of the interests of France on the "*the inferior races*" with a lopsided morality. The uncanny similarity between Mr. Ferry's declaration and a phrase contained in the report of Commission for Africa (Mr. Tony Blair's initiative), released in March 2005 which states that "..the developed world has a moral duty…to assist Africa" constitutes a serious cause for concern.

In some cases, the lopsided morality has been borne on the military might of interest-motivated party as was the recent case in Iraq, the Anglo-Zulu War of 1879, the Islamization of Africa by Arabs and indeed latter day terrorism. In other instances, money and "*trade*" were employed as was the case in the early days of colonialism and present day of "*aid and development*"; and in other cases it has been outright manipulation as is the case with International Monetary Fund and The World Bank.

It is an unfortunate accident of human history that the evil consequences of interests and the lopsided morality of interest-motivated party on their victims take on a permanent form that changes the course of history of the aggrieved party forever. For some peoples, this has led to their near extinction as is the case of original settlers of North American continent and Australia. For the others as is in the case of Africa, it has led to complete dismembering of cultural values, an imperfect definition of the self as individuals or as nations with the concomitant chaos.

The role of the wronged party in providing a field of play for lopsided morality is crucial in the analysis of the entrenchment of associated evil consequences. The response of the wronged party manifests in various forms depending on the approach of the interest-motivated party, but common to all the forms of response is the undermining of the interests of the victims by a select group of their own people, the *mutants*. The emergence of the group of *mutants* or the concept of *mutantism,* a deliberate strategy of the interest-motivated party is founded on concession of certain financial or power privileges to this group. Nigeria's Fela Anikulapo Kuti succinctly describes this phenomenon in his record *ITT (International Thief Thief)*. He says in part:

> "Dem go look for one useless chief
> Dem go give am one million naira bread
> ....the chief go start start im confusion,
> ...start start im oppression....."[18]

Oblivious of the consequences of their collaboration, these *mutants* help entrench the evils of lopsided morality among their peoples. The role of some African traders in the 300 years of slavery is a case in point. Ottobah Cuguano, an African slave in the *Narrative of the Enslavement of a Native of Africa (1787)* said: "But I must own, to the shame of my own countrymen, that I was first kidnapped and betrayed by some of my own complexion, who were the first cause of my exile, and slavery......"[19]. Jean Barbot, in *"A description of the coasts of north and south Guinea, and of Ethiopia...account of the Western maritime countries of Africa"* wrote in 1732 "European traders captured some Africans in raids along the coast but bought most from local African or African-European dealers. They paid the dealers in goods and established regular trading links...."[20] The *mutants* in this case were motivated by financial gains.

In Portuguese and French colonies, *mutants* were given the title of *"assimilated"*. This was a group of Africans *"re-created"* in the "image" of the colonialists. They had been taught to speak the language of the colonialists and imitate their manner. They were given limited privileges and were involved in petty administrative duties within the colonial administration. They served in some instances as the mouthpiece for the colonialists. One could deduce that in this case, the motive of *betrayal*, borrowing the words of Ottobah Cuguano was power and influence.

The foreigner, obsessed with his interests, uses the guise of lopsided morality to occupy, enslave and plunder his victims. In this case, the motive and the guiding sophism are obvious. Contrarily in the case of the *mutants*, while the motives may be clearly known, the moral guise under which they function remains an enigma. There is no doubt that they understand the option of evil, which they have made, and therefore the consequences of their actions on their own people.

Could the morality of the *mutants* be an offshoot of the lopsided morality of their manipulators? The active pursuit and echoing of British Government's intentions by the Zimbabwean opposition leader to effect a regime change of an elected (according to the tenets of Western political philosophy of democracy) government is a clear offshoot of lopsided morality of interest-driven Britain.

Could it have been some other form of morality rooted in some obscure beliefs? An African King, King of Bonny in 1807, in his defense of slave trade, following the Law on Abolition, attributed a divine nature to the practice: "We think this trade must go on. That is the verdict of our oracle and the priests. They say that your country, however great, can never stop a trade ordained by God himself."

Could it have been that the financial and power motives overrode any need to give some moral basis, however lopsided to their actions? This is what King Ghezo of Abomey said of slavery: "The slave trade is the ruling principle of my people. It is the source and the glory of their wealth...the mother lulls the child to sleep with notes of triumph over an enemy reduced to slavery..."

The impact of lopsided morality of interest-driven parties on the wronged party transcends the physical plundering, which is not always very difficult to measure; it creates a new breed of people, a new trait, whose actions are rooted in incomprehensible moral values among the wronged.

A New Trait in the Gene Pool.

o o o o o o o o o o o o o o o o o o o o o o o o o o o o

....we are natural dancers to the music of others....

African history has shown us that Africa has been a bad loser in all its relations with outsiders. Its bane has been blind trust in the spoken, and more recently in the written word of the foreigner and complete obliviousness of the unspoken dark intent.

The ease with which Africans abandoned their values to embrace new ones on contacts with foreigners has been a major contributing factor to the plethora of African problems. Without understanding the motives of the foreigners, Africans to their own detriment have been characterized by their penchant for fanatical adoption of alien ideas and interests.

This easy mutability of values brings under question the conviction of Africans in fundamental traditional self-preserving values. Fundamental self-preserving values do not only ensure survival but also endow dignity and respect. How rooted are these values in governing the behavior of the African as an individual and as a member of a community? Why do these values mutate with each exposure to new and inherently dangerous ideas?

It is an irony of African existence that self-preserving values are sub-ject to spurious changes while destructive and self-abasing ones remain untouched, sometimes untouchable. The mishmash of mutated self-preserving values and untouched self-abasing ones have come to be synonymous with Africa and it is one of the root causes of why the backrow has been *permanently* attributed to the African.

The squandering of resources and values in the face of contacts with other cultures tells the foreigner about the people. He finds willing *mutants* and sows an evil trait among peaceful and trusting people. He learns to manipulate at will and to regard self-preserving values of others as dispensable. This attitude of the foreigner has dogged Africa throughout its history and continues to undermine any genu-ine effort by Africans to redeem themselves. Slavery could not have reached the astronomical dimensions it reached on the African soil, but for the active collaboration of some Africans. Colonialism, divi-sive foreign languages, religion, contrasting ideologies, neo-colonial-ism on the continent all have their roots in the blind embrace of alien ideas, the motives of which are quite unclear to the African.

On embracing these new concepts, the African *mutants* not only facilitate the work of the foreigner, but also give a new twist to the idea in order to strengthen their position thereby condemning their peoples to serve the interest of others. The transmutation of some Africans into rabid slave traders is a reminder of the fickleness of African behavioral convictions. The Smithsonian's African Ameri-can history museum in Washington, D.C. states that while instances of slavery can be found throughout human history, the practice of slavery did not become *"dehumanizing"* until white Europeans came along and took slaves to the Americas. The museum's West Africa exhibit, which opened February 3, 2003, had the following statement at the entrance of the exhibit: "Slavery had existed in Africa as it had in other parts of the world, for centuries, but it was not based on race and it did not result in dehumanization and death, as did transatlantic slavery". Ottobah Cugoano in his *"Narrative of the Enslavement of a Native of Africa"* (1787) gave some credence to the Smithsonian claim. He wrote "So far as I can remember, some of the Africans in my country keep slaves, which they take in war, or for debt; but those which they keep are well fed, and good care taken of them, and treated well......"[21]. Another report states "Many societies in Africa with kings and hierarchical forms of government traditionally kept slaves. But these were mostly used for domestic purposes. They were an indication of power and wealth and not used for commercial gain. However, with the appearance of Europeans desperate to buy slaves for use in the Americas, the character of African slave ownership changed".

So what changed the African?

There is no doubt that the *mutants* developed a new trait in the course of their dealings with the interest-driven foreign partners. In *"An Account of the Slave Trade on the Coast of Africa"* (1788), Alexander Falcolnbridge who had visited Africa in the 1780s described a scene on the African coast. In his words, "When the Negroes whom the black traders have to dispose of are shown to the European purchasers, they first examine them...if they have been afflicted in any manner so as to render them incapable of such labor they are rejected. The traders frequently beat those Negroes which are objected to by the captains. Instances have happened that the traders, when any of their Negroes have been objected to have instantly beheaded them in the sight of the captain"[22].

We know from history that the bricks of the walls of the shrine of Abomey palace of King Ghezo were made with the blood of war captives and slaves.

There is no doubt that a new trait entered the African gene pool in the course of his *alliance* with foreigners. The hitherto humane values of the African were readily replaced with vicious inhuman treatment copied from the foreigner.

This easy transmutation of values, from humane ones as described by the Smithsonian Institute (and attested to by Ottobah Cuguano) to horrendous ones on coming into contact with European slave traders as recorded by Alexander Falconbridge indicates an inherent lability of the convictions of the African in the appropriateness and correctness of his own values.

Could this same reason be responsible for all the problems that Africa faces today? Is it that Africans in power do not see anything wrong with their self-destructive and self-abasing actions and inactions? Is it that they cannot see the enormity of their actions or inactions on black Africans?

Given the power and the financial resources which these *mutants* accrue from their activities, they succeed in constituting themselves into a powerful social group in their societies even after the departure of the initiating external evil force. The power and resources accumulated by this group through the acquisition of this new trait enhances their chances of survival. This trait, which they have put to use in entrenching evil in their society, becomes a dominant survival trait. The tragedy of the mutation is that it erodes the capacity of the mutants to self-criticism. The lack of self-criticism consequent upon the persistence of this trait is a common characteristic among those who should have made a difference in the course of African history and have failed to.

The persistence of this *trait* in the gene pool makes it possible to draw parallels between major actors of early African history and their contemporary counterparts. Mali emperors were known for their extravagant pilgrimages to Mecca, not for their religious zealousness or piety. Mansa Kankan Mussa made the most extravagant pilgrimage to Mecca in African history; he travelled to Mecca in 1325, with 500 slaves and 100 camels (each carrying gold). It is recorded that he gave away gold in enormous quantities to the amazement of all the communities and villages through which he passed. He had gotten the wealth from outrageous taxes on his subjects, levies, sale of slaves, and from enslaving other African states. Robert O. Collins in his African *History, text and readings*, Random House 1971 stated of the rulers of the Mali Empire (1238–1468) that "….although many of these rulers gained fame as a result of their extravagant pilgrimage to Mecca, neither Islamic law nor Islamic social custom was practiced in the Mali Empire…"[23]

Mansa Kankan Mussa has many parallels in contemporary African history. It is a known fact that some post-independence African leaders looted their countries even to the amazement of their greedy Western bankers. African leaders were known and are still famous for their immense ill-gotten wealth and their extravagance in foreign countries, while it is an open secret that their countries are mired in squalor and poverty. Two former African presidents were rated among the ten most corrupt leaders in the world by Transparency International in a report in March 2004: it was claimed that Mobutu Seseko stole about four billion dollars; Nigeria's Sanni Abacha was said to have made away with about six billion dollars. The self-coronated *Emperor* Jean Bokassa of the Central African

Republic made himself a golden *throne* amid the squalor of his country. It is also a known fact that African leaders at all levels of government collude with foreigners to plunder resources from their own countries in order to benefit themselves and deliberately ruin their economy and in their greed sentence their citizens to miserable squalor, disease and dehumanization.

Some form of forced labor and illicit trade in humans still persist in Africa till today. The likes of Babatu, the famous Muslim slave trader, who was born in Niger and conducted his slave raids in Northern Ghana in the 1880's are said to be still thriving more than a century after the abolition of slave trade. Human Rights Watch in its *Background Paper on Slavery and Slavery Redemption in the Sudan* March 1999 reported that "…….abducted children and women often lead lives of extreme deprivation and cruelty at the hands of their masters. Many are physically and sexually abused, and forced to live at a standard well below that of their captors (sleeping on the floor, minimum food, no chance for education). Beatings for "disobedience" are common. They are denied their ethnic heritage, language, religion, and identity as they are cut off from their families and are held by Arabic-speaking captors, most of whom rename the abductees with Arabic names and some of whom coerce the children and women into adopting Islam."[24]

In Mauritania, a large part of the black population, about 30% of the total population of the country are slaves, called the *Haratins.* Slave-ownership is a status symbol among the minority Moor population of this country. Slaves belong to families and are handed down as inheritance. Slavery was officially abolished in Mauritania only in 1981, about a century after the practice was abolished worldwide. This *official abolition,* declared to please the international community does not have any impact on the status of haratins, who continue to remain properties of their masters. *Haratins* have no rights, outside the ones granted them by their masters; they are in bondage and unbelievably, they are still whipped (whatever their age may be) when their masters are displeased with them. They have no identity outside the one granted them by their masters. *Blacks* do not own *Moors* as slaves, *Moors* own *black Africans* as slaves.

One would have expected that the founders of modern Africa in their struggle for independence would have carefully taken into consideration the easy *mutability* of convictions of the African that facilitated atrocities, human tragedies and sufferings on the African soil; and that they would have laid appropriate foundations to discourage the *wastage* of self-preserving values by establishing some minimum standards of norms to guide the African perception of one another. The different forms of atrocities which have been happening on the African soil since independence have proved that African leaders not only failed to see this, but are also inheritors of this repulsive trait.

It is however to the credit of the post apartheid South African government under Thabo Mbeki that they, recognizing that there are some fundamental self-destructive and self-abasing behavioral peculiarities in the African took steps to review the moral code guiding individual behavior in South Africa. On 18 April 2002, the Moral Regeneration Movement was launched in Pretoria by President Thabo Mbeki with 1000 members from all sectors of society including traditional leaders and religions, labor and business, the media and academia, many civil society organizations and NGOs, political parties, and the national, provincial and local government. This is an example worthy of emulation by other responsible African leaders.

The eradication of *mutants or mutantism* from the African society needs to be seen as the *Black Question* that has to be addressed from profound philosophical, religious, political and moral points of view. This is an imperative mission on the success of which the survival, dignity and destiny of the black race lies.

The Trait Managers

o o o o o o o o o o o o o o o o o o o o o o o o o o o o o
...We are in exile,
squeezed between dotted lines,
stamped by those who christened us,
our fathers, who signed away our essence.....

The *mutant* trait has not disappeared from the African gene pool since his first contact with the foreigner. It has been reinventing itself and continually adapting to prevailing circumstances. Given the historical characteristics of this trait as a determinant survival factor, African leaders have in their own interests not only ensured its active survival, but have also employed complicated tools to obfuscate or negate its existence. In their superfluous political discourse, they take the stand of angels bedeviled by others. They invent their own version of history, putting all the responsibility of the cause of problems of Africans on the shoulders of their foreign manipulators. They not only misinform, but also understate or negate what their role and the role of their predecessors as agents of foreign interests have been in the course of African tragic history. They highlight the obvious consequences of African historical experiences and either contort or omit the events leading up to these experiences.

The Charter of the Organization of African Unity founded in 1963 dedicated its Principles to struggle for Independence, respect of sovereignty, non-interference in the affairs of other states and in order to guarantee the survival of these political leaders, in strong terms condemned *political* assassinations. The concern for international cooperation engendered the inclusion of a passing reference to human rights in the charter as it vaguely states under Article II of the Purpose: "To promote international cooperation, having due regard to the Charter of the United Nations and the Universal Declaration of Human Rights". In their quest to consolidate their newly acquired status and the political independence of their erstwhile-colonized "countries", the founders of modern Africa expended tremendous energy and resources in trying to hold together the absurdity of their inheritance of nation-states created by the colonialists. The UN charter on Human Rights was redefined to mean inviolable rights of the ruling class (mutants) and mere lip-service to human rights in political discourse of post-independence African leaders was seen as a legitimate passport to *"international cooperation"*.

Being the first organization of *"liberated"* Africans since the first foreigner set foot on African soil, one would have expected the founding fathers to address the problem of the inherent lability of African behavioral convictions that facilitated the tragedies that befell him. One would have expected the founding fathers to lay down in clear terms minimum standards for guiding the behavior of Africans towards one another as individuals and as a race. This, however, was not to be the case. African founding fathers invested their political energy firstly in confronting the consequences of the historical experiences of the African peoples without paying due regard to events leading up to these experiences. Secondly, in their quest to hold on to power, they employed the same *mutant* trait, the decisive factor in the events leading up to the tragic historical experiences as a political and strategic tool. These two approaches embraced by the founding fathers not only engendered lack of long term vision and a gross misunderstanding of their historical mission but also laid grounds for further atrocities to be committed on African soil. The same vulnerability and lability of behavioral convictions that led to slavery, colonialism and eventually to neocolonialism took its toll on independent Africa. Idi Amin Dada in Uganda, Marcias Nguema in Equatorial Guinea and Jean-Bedel Bokassa in Central African Republic, Mobutu Seseko of Zaire, Jonas Savimbi of Angola, Foday Sankoh of Sierra Leone, Charles Taylor of Liberia, all post-independent African leaders or rebels, either acting on their own or more likely as agents of some foreign manipulating interests unleashed terror of genocidal magnitudes on African peoples. The Organization of African Unity stood mutely by in the name of *non-interference* as these atrocities were committed. Sekou Toure of Guinea summarized this criminal negligence in his famous words that "the OAU is not a tribunal" to bring member countries or their leaders to order.

It is a historical absurdity that the initiative to contain the rampage of the African mutants came, not as an African initiative but under pressure from foreign countries, particularly the United States. The weak attempts by African intellectuals to bring the problem of ethics among Africans to the fore in the sixties were swept under the carpet by the political leaders. Under pressure, (of course linked to withdrawal of aid), the Organization of African Unity began working on a document that would be known as African Charter on Human and Peoples' Rights in 1979. It is to the credit of the then Secretary General of the organization, Mr. Edem Kodjo, that he suggested to the experts charged with drawing up the document to *determine the duties of each person towards the community in which he lives…"*

The Charter, adopted by the OAU in 1981 came into force in 1986, some 38 years after the creation of the United Nations Charter on Human Rights. One of the clauses of the preamble of the African Charter interestingly states "Taking into consideration the virtues of their historical tradition and the values of African civilization which should inspire and characterize their reflection on the concept of human and peoples' rights.." It is logical to ask what values and historical tradition this preamble is making reference to in the face of African history. The most widely known consequences of African values and historical tradition have been the participation of some Africans in the subjugation of African peoples and subsequent relegation of Africa to the rear in the human march to greatness. This preamble does not reflect our reality, or our history, it is a contradiction of our historical facts.

The Charter in its Article 5 states in part that ".....All forms of exploitation and degradation of man particularly slavery, slave trade, torture, cruel, inhuman or degrading punishment and treatment shall be prohibited". The continued existence of slavery in Sudan, Niger, Mauritania, and the atrocities that happened in wars under different guises in Nigeria, Mozambique, Angola, Rwanda, Zaire, Congo, Ethiopia, Guinea Bissau, Burundi, Somalia, Liberia, Sierra Leone and Ivory Coast after the Charter came into force are indications that the fundamental flaw in our perception of one another that characterized the slavery period still haunts the African psyche, and that this Charter is only a signboard of good intentions, a product without a market.

One is indeed tempted to ask if the behavior of Africans towards one another has really changed since slavery times. The much contested and detested exemption of Africans from historical development by Hegel in his *Philosophy of History*, stating that their "condition is capable of no development of culture, and as we see them at this day, such they have always been.."[25] seems more of a curse on Africans than philosophy. Even the Vatican in 18th century believed that Africa was under a curse. There was a doctrine that Black Africans were the accursed sons of Ham (Genesis 9: 18-27).

The Negritude movement which sought to negate this Hegelian and other "*curses*" and affirm pride in black heritage and culture, did not really have any tangible reference from Africa, save the need to negate the stigma and affirm that the black race belonged to the human race whatever its shortcomings might have been. They would find the only reference in the commonness of sufferings and the color of the skin. Oruno Lara lamented «…. we seem to have neither a past, nor civil status, it was up to…. us to edify a more beautiful past, drawing upon our heritage of sacrifice and pro-bity."[26]

Ironically, we have always been told that others have been and are responsible for our problems, and that those that are responsible have some degree of *moral responsibility* (which means financial responsibility) to find solutions to the myriad of problems that Black Africa is confronted with. It is misleading to continue to teach African children that others have been and are responsible for the present state of Africa. Africans need to be truthful to themselves and by so doing begin the process of honest self-examination in order to be able to lay the foundations for solving their problems and leaving a decent legacy for future generation of Africans. African leaders should desist from looking for solutions to problems which are inherently African from outside. In the words of Anton Lebede, a South African political activist "no one other than the Africans can free Africans…." This, they can only do when they openly and honestly engage in ridding themselves of their obnoxious inherited *mutant* trait that has dogged the African society for more than eight hundred years.

African leaders could learn from Yevgeny Chevchenko, a Russian poet, who inadvertently but succinctly warns this generation of African leaders in his poem *"Lies"*:

> "Telling lies to the young is wrong....
> ....Forgive no error you recognize,
> it will repeat itself, increase,
> and afterwards our pupils
> will not forgive in us what we forgave"[27]

Occupying the Mind

○ ○

"The most powerful weapon in the hands of the oppressor is the mind of the oppressed"

—*Steven Biko.*

Why is Africa different from other colonized cultures?

Africans are not the only peoples in the world to have been colonized. But something sets Africa apart. Some incomprehensible vulnerability factor. Some strange loyalty to their past or present occupying and oppressive forces. An *algophilic* hedonistic yearning that seems to pull Africans continuously towards their historical and new sources of pains.

Any land could be occupied; any nation could be colonized under the flimsiest of excuses. The occupying force cannot however not be contented with occupying only the land, he actively seeks to re-engineer the mind of the oppressed peoples. The objective of the occupying force is dual in this regard. He seeks the mind of his victims not only to concede him legitimacy but also to make them see themselves through his own eyes. He seeks to re-create them in his own image by imposing his language as the official language of communication, his religion, his culture. In the words of Ngugi wa

Thiong'o, he *"dis-members"* their way of life, their perception of themselves and *"re-members"* them in his own image. He seeks to create an imperfect version of himself, a clone amenable to the dictates of his short and long-term objectives of plundering.

In seeking to liberate themselves, oppressed people will be compelled to conduct their struggle on two fronts: liberation of their land and liberation of their mind. The order in which these struggles are conducted will determine the characteristics of the future liberated nation. The choice of the order of the struggles and the methods chosen to conduct them become enormous historical responsibility on the avant-garde intelligentsia and the political class of the oppressed peoples. Where the choice of freeing the mind before freeing the land is made, the avant-garde intelligentsia and the political elite are obliged to carefully examine the fundamental lapses and weaknesses that in the first place made the oppressed people vulnerable to occupation and exploitation from which they are seeking to liberate themselves. This analysis should not be conducted within the framework of any foreign ideology, but within the context of cultural and ethical peculiarities of the people concerned. There should be a deliberate policy to purge the people's mind of the occupier's pervasive hold and *re-re-member* it to its near original state.

The liberation of the land, when it comes, will find an experienced people who will seek to correct the socio-cultural weaknesses that made them vulnerable to occupation and oppression. Under this order of liberation struggle, the superiority of individual, ethnic and religious identities over the legacy of the occupying force's flawed institution becomes obvious. The common recognition of the inherently divisive and the contradictory nature of the oppressor's amorphous institutions will constitute the basis for a peaceful reorganization of the society based on mutual understanding and inter-ests. Undoing the damage inflicted by the oppressor will in this case not be a painful process.

Frantz Fanon, a French-Antilles born Algerian psychiatrist in his book *The Wretched of the Earth* (1961) recognized the uncondi-tional need of the oppressed to achieve mental liberation from the humiliation which the oppressors have institutionalized into a way of life. The violent method and the apparent Marxist platform from which he proposed to do this were faulted with inherent contradic-tion of discarding one way of life, based on one alien philosophy and replacing it with another founded on another alien philosophy. The advocacy of violence to achieve this psychological liberation was in principle counterproductive to the oppressed peoples' psyche and cause. It encouraged a culture of violence and directly conferred legitimacy on violence as an acceptable method of effecting social change.

In the case where the choice of liberation of the land precedes the liberation of the mind, it is generally taken for granted that the lib-eration of the mind is a *fait accompli* in the event of a political liber-ation. This assumption is founded on the illusory premise that the openly manifested desire of the victims to rid themselves of their oppressors could be equated to the liberation of the mind. The open manifestation to physically eject the oppressors, which is an expres-sion of a long-held subconscious desire to invert power relations since the arrival of the occupying force is erroneously taken by the liberation movement avant-garde as an expression of the liberation of the mind. The conditions for revolution will thus appear to have matured. The crack, inflicted on the superstructure of the occupa-tion by the local rebellion and the effects of other favorable socio-political events in other parts of the world will further convince the avant-garde of the accuracy of their interpretation. The urgency of expelling the occupying force informs the search for an ideological base to conduct the struggle.

In most of Africa, Marxist ideology became the strategy of choice. The Marxist class struggle theory as a platform of analysis was not only a gross misunderstanding of underlying causes of the occupation and its long duration, but also constituted a deliberate dismissal of the historical and socio-cultural peculiarities of the oppressed that favored the occupation and oppression.

The nebulous assumption of the universality and applicability of the dialectical causes of an in-*country* social repression to liberation struggles from a foreign occupying power constitutes an intellectual misjudgment and a historical injustice to the oppressed peoples of the occupied nation. This assumption inherently sentences the oppressed peoples to view themselves through the mirror of others with whom they do not share the same course of history or the same circumstances of vulnerability. The intelligentsia and the political class convinced of their approach limit their perception and indeed their perceptibility to an inappropriate and potentially damaging ideological scope. The liberators and their followers are compelled to lose their identity within one common one-size-fits-all strategy both as a diagnostic tool and as a remedial antidote to their vulnerability. Consequently, much energy is directed at imposing the dictates of this strategy as a post-liberation development tool without regard for the socio-cultural characteristics of the liberated people. This major lapse will later spell disaster not only for the liberated peoples but also for their liberators. The liberators' misunderstanding of the profundity of divisive strategy of the occupying power and their misguided conviction that profound historical injustices and atrocities could be corrected with another foreign ideology that *uniformizes* perception of the self as members of a class within the confines of a foreign-imposed border will later spell doom.

Under this new dispensation, the *liberated* peoples are obliged to move from one form of incomprehensible mental re-engineering to another form in which their yearnings for individual, ethnic and religious identities would later be dubbed as reactionary. The pervasive strategy and tools of enforcement of the erstwhile colonial oppressors come handy for the liberators, not only to keep themselves in power, but to check the natural tendencies of the peoples to find their solutions.

In the case of Africa, the leaders in the post-independence period not only enforced these tools but made them sacrosanct. In the preamble to The Organization of African Unity Charter of 1963 African leaders actually declared that they were "determined to safeguard and consolidate the hard-won independence as well as the sovereignty and territorial integrity of our states....". The colonial structural and mental re-engineering legacy of incongruous borders, language, administration, religion and culture thus became permanent features of Africa.

In the absence of vision and ideas, African liberator-leaders held on dearly to their colonial legacy; and indeed transformed it into a status symbol. The more profound the mental re-engineering, the more sophisticated they portrayed themselves flaunting their short umbilical ties with their former oppressors. This short umbilical connection otherwise known as *"historical ties"* of the oppressed to his oppressor, the self-abasing *algophilic* hedonism not only deludes the oppressed into a false sense of common identity with his oppressor, but also serves as the Grail of discrimination against other Africans of different mental re-engineering and color of umbilical cords.

Thus, African francophones see themselves as having more in common with the French than with their African anglophone "brothers", who also see themselves as kin of English speaking Western countries with nothing in common with their francophone neighbors. The lusophones stand world apart too, their brothers being the Portuguese. The mental re-engineering process begun in the 15th century would have borne fruits. The primordial connection of traditions, culture and color, the common history of injustice, subjugation and humiliation become insignificant in the re-invented African.

It is lamentable that African leaders go out of their ways as a sign of prestige to belong to organizations (language schools) of former occupied countries like the so called Commonwealth, the CPLP (community of Portuguese speaking countries), the Francophonie. In their minds, it is a shame not to belong to these bodies, and they fight hard to retain their seat when they are threatened to be expelled like school boys from these bodies. They have failed to see these bodies as a reminder of the tragedy that befell us as peoples in 1884/1885. Whatever benefits they think they reap from making us belong to these bodies should be weighed against the indignity and the humiliations of the historical *raison d'être* of these bodies.

African Borders

The sacredness of any border or frontier created by an occupying force should come under question after the liberation of the oppressed people. The subconscious desire of the victims for a natural re-arrangement premised on their socio-cultural identities must be given expression by their leaders. It is the responsibility of the political leaders to consciously forgo their personal ambition of occupying the seats vacated by the oppressors. This is the height of selflessness in the service of the people and a potent foundation in the march to completely dismantle the dehumanizing legacy of herding Africans behind obnoxious colonial lines called borders.

Unfortunately, the founding fathers of *liberated* Africa maintained a post-liberation policy of maintaining the inviolability of these absurd and unnatural borders. In their ambition to occupy the seat of their erstwhile oppressors, they failed to see their *"territory"* not only as a reminder of a historical injustice and humiliation, but also as an undermining factor of a concerted development of the black race. The Organization of African Unity in its charter even declared these frontiers as sacred and inviolable!

The borders of modern Africa were arbitrarily drawn by a group of 13 European countries and the USA in the Berlin conference of 1884/1885. The borders were drawn in the absence of Africans, and as usual the interest of the African did not figure on the minds of any of these countries. These borders were drawn to serve the interests of these European countries to the complete disregard of the diversity of cultural, ethnic and traditional interests of African peoples. African people who had hitherto been members of the same community or village suddenly found themselves on different sides of the border, governed by two groups of Europeans speaking different languages!

The Fulanis of northern Nigeria who have much more in common with the Peulh of the Sahel will find themselves lumped with the Igbos and the Efiks of the West African coast in an entity called Nigeria. The Makondes in the north of Mozambique who share the same culture and tradition with the Makondes of southern Tanzania are lumped with the Rongas of Maputo, who on their part share very similar history, culture and tradition with the Zulus of South Africa. The geographical absurdities of Senegal and Gambia, Congo, Rwanda, Burundi and Uganda confound a rational mind. Matt. T. Rosenberg in his article, *Berlin Conference of 1884–1885 to Divide Africa—The Colonization of the Continent by Colonial Powers* wrote "......At the time of the conference, 80% of Africa remained under traditional and local control. What ultimately resulted was a hodgepodge of geometric boundaries that divided Africa into fifty-four irregular countries. This new map of the continent was superimposed over the one thousand indigenous cultures and regions of Africa. The new countries lacked rhyme or reason and divided coherent groups of people and merged together disparate groups who really did not get along........".[28] The carving of these borders served only the interests of the countries at the Berlin conference and excluded any African interest. Since post-independence period, these borders have been sources of major disputes among many African countries.

Why do African leaders continue to hold sacrosanct these borders that were carved out in other peoples' interests? Who gains from this atrocious act? Those that gained from it have supposedly left after "independence"; why maintain them? Whom are our leaders afraid of? Keeping these borders is an indication of the unwillingness of African leaders to undo a despicable legacy. One could only imagine that only they and their foreign masters benefit from this travesty of "countries".

African Brothers

o o o o o o o o o o o o o o o o o o o o o o o o o o o

"…the advocates of colonialism laugh to themselves derisively when they hear magnificent declarations about African unity"

—*Frantz Fanon*

Joseph Ndiaye, the curator of the *"Maison des esclaves"* in Goree Island in Senegal in his presentation of the museum to visitors likes to emphasize the indignity of the immediate loss of identity of those rounded off to be sold. He tells the visitors to the museum of how slaves immediately lost their names and were given new names by their buyers; how members of the same family sold off to different buyers acquired different identities before being shipped to different parts of the world. In distant lands, slaves from different back-grounds belonging to the same owner were identified under the umbrella identity given to them by their *owner.*

The commonness of suffering, the feeling of individual rootlessness in a foreign land and the natural human need for a sense of belong-ing, an identity, even as it were, of common victim-hood served as a catalyst of unity among blacks taken away into slavery. They came to regard each other as brothers and sisters, bound together by their yearnings for freedom and dignity. The Diaspora thus gave Africa its first lesson on pan-negrist unity; that common interests in seeking self-esteem and liberty transcended plantation owners' identity tags; and in the case of Africa, should transcend divisive borders, languages and religions.

The African Diaspora played a foundational role in introducing pan-Africanist ideology to future African leaders as a means of redeeming the dignity of the black race. The Diaspora sought a proud reference in black Africa, a strong antidote to their humiliation; a place of refuge from the travails of foreign lands. They groomed and influenced some future African leaders and the idea of Pan-Africanism became a political philosophy, not only to advance the cause of Africa and but also to provide the African Diaspora with some tangible reference. Kwame Nkrumah was a notable and influential African politician who attempted to put this philosophy into practice. He was subsequently demonized by those who felt threatened and who still feel threatened by the idea of a unified Africa.

Under unseen but ever-present manipulative hands, with active participation of African agents, the Pan-Africanist philosophy slowly underwent a slow mutation devoid of its essence on African soil. Now it is fashionable for African leaders to refer to one another as brothers without giving a thought to the meaning or intending to act on the idea. Individual selfish and *"national"* interests and the *"historical ties"* have confined this philosophy to history books. It is not unusual in Africa to see mortal warring factions who have been brought together under the auspices of *"peacemakers"* to discuss peace, referring to each other in these meetings as brothers, only to come back to Africa, pick up their arms and continue their combat.

The supreme body for African interest is commonly accepted to be the African Union, where example of real unity, brotherhood and understanding of one another is supposed to be shown to all Africans. The integrity and dignity of Africans peoples are supposed to be superior to all individual and *"historical ties"* interests. The conduct of some African leaders during the second African Union Meeting which was held in Maputo, Mozambique in 2003 said a lot about the prospects of African unity. This august meeting was disrupted to the consent of some African leaders by a five day visit of the American president to five African countries. It was indeed a surprise to see African leaders scuttling out of Maputo to rush back to their countries to receive the visitor and in turn ruin what might have turned out to be their legacy to future generations of Africans. The American President did not want to meet the leaders as a group in Maputo. The chosen ones felt privileged. They conceded to disrupt the meeting. The American President simply put the so called unity to test, and of course, what does not exist cannot stand any test. The so called unity has never existed and does not exist, and it failed the simplest of tests.

Not wanting to be left behind in undermining whatever visions the African Union, NEPAD or indeed any gathering of Africans (set up to address the problems facing the continent) have, Mr. Tony Blair, the British Prime Minister decided as a *personal initiative* to set up what was labeled Commission for Africa, charged to provide "a comprehensive assessment of the situation in Africa...what has worked and what has not worked and what more can and should be done". In October 2004, African intellectuals from within Africa and the Diaspora, together with African politicians were gathered in Dakar at the instance of the African Union to discuss the problems facing the continent and propose ways to build African capacity and self-reliance. Like the American president did the year before, the

British Prime Minister chose the exact moment to fly to Addis Ababa to attend the meeting of his Commission for Africa. Obviously in the eyes of the Prime Minister, the august Dakar gathering was worth much less than his *personal initiative* group of seventeen people of whom eight were non-Africans.

Whatever the intentions of the Commission are, the timing of its October 2004 meeting, which was uncannily reminiscent of the timing of American president's visit to Africa the previous year, speaks volumes. Rather than support the African initiatives embodied by NEPAD and the African Union, the Blair Commission is attempting to employ the age-old tactics of divide and rule by creating a parallel structure and solution to undermine home grown initiatives. In its report released in March, 2005, the commissioners acknowledged that Africans have not been folding their arms too. They declared "And Africa—at country, regional, and continental levels—is creating much stronger foundations for tackling its problems. Recent years have seen improvements in economic growth and in governance"[29]. So, if this were so, one would like to ask what the essence of a parallel solution based on "personal initiative" of a non-African is. Could he possibly love Africa more than Africans?

If the long-term intentions and proposed solutions of this Commission are not understood now, as had been many other obscure foreign-born initiatives to *"assist"* Africa before it, history has taught us that unsolicited *"initiatives"* and *"assistance"* are at best detrimental to the cause of Africa and are only conceived to serve the long term interests of their initiators. The African Union has a duty to view this *"personal initiative"* and its recommendations not only against the backdrop of its parallel and inherently distractive nature, but also against its potential capacity to undermine the charted course of development defined by African Union and NEPAD.

If the plight and the humiliation of the African in the world is not understood because it becomes formless in the smoke of political discourse between our leaders and foreign leaders; if our leaders fail to see that our condition rubs off on them and says a lot about them despite red-carpet receptions which they receive in foreign countries; if they fail to see that dignity is not bestowed by photo sessions with their foreign counterparts, but by their recognized effort to redeem African peoples from the humiliation of their conditions; if they fail to understand that *normal* political leaders fight for the interest of their people and nations, not their personal interests, at least they should be able to see that there is a calculated attempt to undermine any prospects of African unity. They should understand the enormity of history on their shoulders and move from century-old (since first pan-Africanist conference of 1900) rhetoric to the action of uniting Africans.

The African Intelligentsia

One is inclined to question what has been the role of African philosophers and thinkers in deciphering what are the underlying problems that make Africa so vulnerable to all forms of manipulation and make of it a compliant field of atrocities and tragedies. What solutions have been proposed and how feasible are these solutions? How do these solutions address the fundamental problem of lability of behavioral convictions? What has been their role in redeeming the dignity of the African who has been persecuted throughout most of his history?

Black intellectuals on African soil and in Diaspora have for more than a century been proposing different theories directed not only at the emancipation of black peoples, but also directed at redeeming the dignity of the black race. These Black African intellectuals have however been influenced mostly by the prevailing circumstances and the period in which they found themselves. Their perception of the problems and the solutions they have proposed to these problems have been shaped by their experiences as Agostinho Neto explicitly formulated "…..it is natural that it should be thus, since our consciousness cannot draw upon material to form itself except from the field of lived experience…."[30].

The oppression of blacks in the British colonies and the oppression of blacks in post-abolition period in the United States gave rise to organized black emancipation movements. These associations and movements like W.E.B. Du Bois' *National Association for the Advancement of Colored People*, the *Harlem Renaissance*, Marcus Garvey's *Universal Negro Improvement Association* (UNIA), the *African Communities League* and the *Back to Africa* movement constituted the first nudge to wake Africa from its self-induced trance of humanity's martyrdom. Africa was called upon by the Diaspora to take up its historical responsibility of providing a proud reference for all blacks in the world.

In 1900, the first Pan-Africanist conference was organized in London by Henry Sylvester Williams, a lawyer from Trinidad. W.E.B Du Bois played an active role in subsequent organization of Pan-Africanist congresses between 1919 and 1927. The aims of these movements were directed at liberation of colonies, emancipation of blacks and in the case of Marcus Garvey's *"Back to Africa"* movement, at encouraging blacks in Diaspora, particularly in the United States to return back to Africa

The contact of some future African leaders like Kwame Nkrumah, Jomo Kenyatta, Hastings Kamuzu Banda, Sekou Toure with these activities later strongly influenced their involvement in liberation movements in Africa and guided their political philosophy. Kwame Nkrumah became a key figure in the organization of the fifth Pan African conference in 1945. Leopold Sedar Senghor and Aimé Cesaire provided a French version of the black consciousness movement in *Negritude*, a philosophy that sought to promote cultural heritage of the black race in Africa and in diaspora. Negritude sought to put values on all things of black origin, actively contesting Hegelian declaration that the black race's "condition is capable of no development of culture".

While these movements provided the cause for the Africans to liberate the colonies, Marxist socialist ideology provided the direction for most African countries during this period. The struggle for African independence was thus conducted with ideological and cultural undertones that marked the political orientation of post independence Black Africa.

The polarity of the world into two ideologically opposing power blocs had a lot of influence on the perception of the problems of Africa and hence, the solutions proffered by African intellectuals. In the words of Agostinho Neto, the view of African problems and the methods to overcome them could not be "..dissociated from acquired political ideas, from ideological positions..."[31].

The prevailing circumstances of these periods influenced the perception of Black African problems by emerging African leaders. The problems were seen as direct consequences of the actions of others, that is, the colonialists. Consequently, a tremendous amount of African intellectual energy was directed at combating the political philosophy of the oppressors. Inadequate efforts were directed at self-examination and self-criticism. Questions were not asked on what made the Black African susceptible to the injustices which these leaders and intellectuals had to fight against. The effect rather than the cause of vulnerability of the African dominated the discourse.

The political independence of Africa, which later came, whether as a direct result of political and philosophical activism of Africans or as the first steps of a new long-term strategy of the colonialists, in a way convinced the founding fathers of modern Africa and the intellectuals of the period of the relevance and pertinence of their approach. In the euphoria of political independence, massive social re-engineering based upon the ideological leanings of the leaders was embarked upon. This social re-engineering which took the convictions, attitude and behavior of the common man for granted soon ran into difficulties. This proved that in the course of liberation struggle, little attention was paid to the mindset and the aspirations of the common man as an individual and as a member of the community at large.

While the leaders sought to use the abstract form of governance inherited from the colonialists and alien ideology to reinvent their societies, the common man sought to do away with this intangible system that had governed his life. This divergence in the outlook of the leaders and the people was eventually exploited either by foreign interests or by their African agents to destabilize the polity in form of military coups, civil disobedience, or outright wars.

The reaction of the leaders to this divergence of views led to unprecedented human rights abuses and great loss of life in post-independence Africa. These excesses led to the emergence of a new breed of African intellectuals whose energy was directed at challenging the human rights abuses of African leaders. A permanent schism thus appeared between the African political class and the African intelligentsia. The voice of dissent of the African intellectual, not directed this time at the erstwhile foreign oppressors, would find loud echo in foreign lands. As was the case during liberation struggles, the intellectual energy of the African intelligentsia was wholly directed at the injustices perpetrated by the political class and not at the cause of vulnerability of the common man.

The cause of this vulnerability came to be viewed and continues to be defined by foreign pundits and some African intellectuals as poverty, illiteracy and disease among a host of other possible ills. As was the case with pre-independence struggles where political liberation was the *raison* and foreign ideology provided the direction, *liberation* from vulnerability has become the *raison* and foreign-born development provides the "*direction*".

Africa in its recent history has again failed to see that solutions to the problem of vulnerability of the African cannot be found in foreign-conceived ideas or ideologies.

The root cause of the vulnerability of the African to manipulation, subjugation, humiliation and oppression cannot be addressed from a foreign politico-economic or philosophical point of view. Even the mere negation of these views in the analysis of African problems would be in the words of W.E.B. Du Bois, to see "..one's self through the eyes of others,...measuring one's soul by the tape of a world that looks on in amused contempt and pity"[32]. The diagnosis of the African problem of vulnerability and the solution to this problem should be founded only and purely on the African existential experience and this exercise must be conducted only by black people from all spheres of life.

The vulnerability of the African and the consequences there-from is entrenched in his perception of himself, his relationship with his gods, his view of the world around him and his nature-given, incurable openness and trust of those who do not look like him believing blindly that they have his interest at heart.

Religiosity: Root of Vulnerability

There is no doubt that the African is innately religious.

Numerous books and articles have been written on the religiosity of the black African, his perception of the world around him, the universal black African belief in one Supreme Being, the existence of lesser gods and his ancestral spirits. The world, according to the African is divided between the visible and the invisible; human beings and God and the spirits with continuous interaction between the two. The invisible takes on the role of protection of the visible; while the visible worships and strives to please the invisible.

While the Supreme Being is not depicted in any physical form in Black Africa, the lesser gods, intercessors between the man and the Supreme Being are depicted in various physical forms and are worshipped and regularly consulted, either through divinations or trances. The division of the lesser gods into gods that govern material elements like rivers, the sea, mountain, iron, lightning etc. and those of mythical origins like the devil, god of twins, gods that control certain illnesses provides a wide range of worship-able deities with different rituals. Different families or clans within the same community may worship different deities. To this diversity is added the worship of ancestral spirits which is even more clan-specific. The existence of this plethora of worship-able deities suggests that religiosity is an important component of the socio-cultural life of an African.

The interaction of the people with these different deities manifests in physical forms through rituals and sacrifices and in spiritual forms through divinations. This interaction is guided by a set of beliefs and norms that are enforced by the cult of the deity concerned. These beliefs and norms dictate the values, ethics, traditional laws, customs and taboos of the followers of this deity. The infringement of any of the norms is believed to provoke the displeasure of the deity which may inflict punishment on the individual, the clan or the community. The punishment, which depends on the deity concerned, may vary from bad luck, illness and death to communal catastrophes like drought, flooding and wars. In such circumstances, the offended deity is consulted by the diviners and appropriate propitiation would be demanded of the offenders. The ancestral spirits which are believed to protect the family or the clan also have the appropriate rituals which are clan-specific.

The contact of the Black African with Arab traders and the introduction of Islam, and the subsequent arrival of Western Christian missionaries introduced a new dimension into African religiosity. These religions with their Monotheistic concepts converted either by convincing or by coercion to their "new" ways. The African "convert" from whom according to some scholars, the idea of one supreme being had originated since the time of Nefertiti, long before Moses was born in Egypt, went along but then reserved his being to his gods. Diedrich Westermann in his *Africa and Christianity* (Oxford University Press, 1937) remarked on this attitude of the West African to the imported God as being "…no more than a Platonic acknowledgement….."[33]. The African was not without his gods and his Supreme Being before the arrival of foreigners on its shores, but since he had nothing to lose by going along with a new concept, he might as well follow it.

Pope Paul VI, realizing that despite the enthusiastic profession of Catholic faith by Africans the adherents still held on steadfastly to their gods and traditions acknowledged the relevance of African Traditional religions in the life of the African in his *Africae Terrarum* of October 1967. He conceded that "many customs and rites, once considered to be strange are seen today, in the light of ethnological science, as integral parts of various social systems, worthy of study and commanding respect. In this regard, we think it profitable to dwell on some general ideas which typify ancient African religious cultures because we think their moral and religious values deserving of attentive consideration"[34]. And Pope John Paul II in his *Ecclesia in Africa* also acknowledged that "..Africans have a profound religious sense, a sense of the sacred, of the existence of God the creator and of a spiritual world.."[35]

On the Islam front, Ibn Battuta (1304–1368) during his travel across Mali circa 1352 noted that "negroes are very zealous in their attempt to learn the holy Quran by heart" and Robert O. Collins in his *African History*, Random House 1971 countered that while the rulers of Mali Empire (1238–1468) "gained fame as a result of their extravagant pilgrimage to Mecca, neither Islamic law nor Islamic social custom was practiced in the Mali Empire"[36].

The African held steadfastly to his beliefs and his gods despite all the onslaughts to convince him to abandon them and imported world religions have had to africanize.

Against this background of the known black African attitude of *"platonic acknowledgement of God"*, the emotions and paparazzi that accompany the Swearing of Oath of office by African public office holders, whereby they *solemnly* place their hands either on the Bible or Quoran, *swearing* to uphold the constitution of their country and respect the ethics of their office constitute a travesty of any solemn ceremony. It is a superfluous parody invented to satisfy implacable adherents of protocol and to reassure the *international community* of conformity to *international norms*. It is a theatrical *acceptance* of a contractual engagement, a make-believe ceremony where the contractee knows that he is not under any obligation to carry out the terms of the contract, because he is not bound by any oath which he recognizes.

Unsurprisingly to all but the most self-deluding Westernized African, he actively flouts the letter of the contract (constitution) which he has *"vowed"* to uphold and disregards the responsibility of his office. The theatre becomes even more hilarious, when the same public office holder enjoins his citizens to fast and pray (in churches and mosques) to ward off the socio-economic tragedies which his dereliction of duties has unleashed on the citizens.

The performance of the African public office holder would probably be different if on taking up an office, they were obliged to swear on the traditional gods of their clan or their ethnic groups. The fear of the reprisals of these gods if he transgresses is more real to him than any other form of enforcement of his contractual obligations to his people.

Spirituality and Relational Dynamics

When the self-inflicted calamities that have been bedeviling black Africa are projected against the background of the religiosity of its people, one is inclined to ask what has been the role of religion in the ethics, outlook and behavior of the black African in the course of his difficult history? How could people of such deep religious convictions have either participated of their own free will or have been coerced into participating in the engineering of their own near extinction?

How could Africans collaborate with slave traders?
How could Africans sell off other Africans?
How could Africans collaborate with colonialists?
How could Africans be known for senseless internecine wars?
How could corruption become a trademark of Africa?
How could poverty become synonymous with Africa despite enormous resources on the continent?
How could Africa be perceived by others as *"the festering disaster of our age"*?

It is an accepted fact that religions, both African traditional religions and adopted alien ones practiced in Africa, are founded on spirituality and on certain ethical and moral values either dictated by The

Book or transmitted through oral tradition as obligations and taboos.

Spirituality constitutes a very important aspect of the religiosity of the African. This spirituality based on African traditional beliefs is innate and does not change with exposure to other cultures. The ethics and code of conduct associated with the beliefs of the African are however subject to change depending on the prevailing circumstances. On exposure to other religions, the associated ethics and code of conduct of the new religion are forcefully blended with values and ethics dictated by African traditional beliefs. The inherent contradictory nature of these hybrids of values and ethics becomes a source of confusion for the African. In the case of Catholicism, Pope Paul V1, recognizing this trend, exhorted Africans to "have an African Christianity" based on African "human values and characteristic forms of culture….". In other words, he advised Africans to structure the hybrids of ethics and values in forms, founded on their own perception of themselves. This challenge only translated into a modification of form of worship (introduction of drums and dances into churches with accompanying dances reminiscent of any traditional worship) and not into development of new values or ethics.

In order to save himself from the confusion of blending alien and traditional values, the African deftly leaves the problem of values aside and holds on dearly to his spirituality. Moreover, spirituality acquires a more important and an influencing role in his religiosity and hence in his behavior. The large dimension taken up by spirituality within the whole sphere of the religiosity of the African informs the behavior of the African as an individual and as a member of a community.

Values and ethics either as direct or indirect derivatives of religiosity, together with spirituality constitute the foundation of relational dynamics within any society.

The *relational* dynamics within any society and therefore the functioning of the society could be imagined as a closed system of energy with a shape of an inverted "T". The energy contained in this relational system is the total sum of mental, physical and spiritual energies of all the members of the given society. It is inherent in the society and cannot be added to or subtracted from by any outside influences. The much flaunted secularism or separation of the state from the church or mosque seeks to break this energy system into its individual components. This, from my point of view is an impossible task, no matter what the level of development of consciousness of the society might be. The redistribution of this energy is however a possible and necessary endeavor for the cohesiveness of the society and the safeguarding of the rights and interests of its citizens.

The vertical bar in the inverted "T" symbolizes spirituality, the relationship with God or the spirits' realm; while the horizontal bar symbolizes the relationship with the environment as defined by the ethics and morals of the religion concerned. This relationship with the environment could be defined as the relationship within and between groups of individuals either as families, clans, tribes or race and the milieu in which they function.

The amount of energy *subconsciously* attributed by a given society to each of the bars will determine the shape of this inverted "T", and therefore determine the way that society functions. It is these dynamics that determines the progress or not of a society.

Many would argue that an ideal society would be one where the energy is equally distributed between the vertical and horizontal bars. This society could be defined as a spiritual and a *just* one. *"Just"* in this case means a *natural inclination* based on individual convictions to do good, to choose good over evil in their interactions with others or *"Just"* as may be arrived at through the conscious, but less reliable imposed rule of law. Under such impositions of rule of law, people live under a conscious or subconscious fear of litigations or of law enforcement authorities. A *"breakdown of law and order"* comes quickly in the wake of natural or man-made events that tend to overwhelm the law enforcement capacities of these societies.

In societies where more energy is subconsciously attributed to the horizontal bar, and therefore, a concomitant feeble vertical bar (probably the so called secular states), people tend to be less spiritual and their energy is invested in the creation of a *just* society.

Societies that are characterized by a strong vertical bar and less pronounced horizontal bar, tend to be more spiritual; with the attendant consequence of less available energy to invest in the creation of a just society. The feeble horizontal bar could only function within a limited range before it is expended. This limited range may be the family or the clan or in some instances the ethnic group.

In Africa, spirituality in whichever form it is expressed occupies a predominant role in the whole spectrum of African religiosity; the vertical bar is overcharged with energy and the scope of action of the horizontal energy bar becomes limited to families, clans and exceptionally to ethnic groups.

When Africa is viewed against this background, the root of the historical tragedy that befell the black African and the plethora of problems that he faces become easier to understand. The reason for the active involvement of Africans in slavery, the cycles of internecine massacres, corruption and concerted efforts to advance the course of the black race comes into clear perspective. The applicability or not of proffered solutions both local and imported becomes apparent. The futility of the assumption that all African problems would disappear under the blanket solution of development also becomes evident.

In the face of the problems (that are premised on religiosity) which the continent faces, it is an irony that Africans in their search for solutions to political and economic problems are tending to become more religious, more spiritual. Religion in all its forms has become a huge industry in Africa in the last two decades. The religious *"international community"* has also been very active in spiritualizing the African through their *"aid"* in the construction of mosques, churches, synagogues and other places of worship. The political *"international community"* on the other hand proposes Western democracy borne on aid or sometime military might as a solution to what apparently is not a political problem. There is no doubt that these imported solutions, which have become the vogue today and have found active apologists even among African intellectuals will not only fail to bring about the African renaissance and dignity, rather, they will complicate the problems and make any possibilities of the emergence of appropriate home-grown solutions by Africans more remote and unattainable.

The dubious motive of foreign governments' *assistance* and *aid* to Africa becomes evident when the relational energy dynamics within the societies of these donor countries is taken into consideration. It will be self-deceit to imagine that these donor countries have excess energy in their horizontal bars to spread beyond their borders. The situation of minorities in these countries shows that these donor countries *do need* their horizontal energy to create more just societies. Given the rate and the ferocity at which they try to outdo each other in their political discourse to give *"aid"* to Africa, to heal the *"festering sore"* of their age, their real motive as regards Africa should come under serious scrutiny.

It is clear that the donor countries intend to expend or more rightly invest in Africa some of the energy in their horizontal bar of which they obviously do not have enough. When their *assistance* and *aid* are viewed through the myopic lengths of short-term gains, African leaders are deceived into the altruism of these *aids* and *assistance*; but when one takes a careful look at the long-term implications of these *aids* and *assistance*, then it becomes clear that Africa should shut its doors to these manacling gestures. They are horizontal bar energy loans, which Africa will have to pay back several times over.

The problems that face Africa are symptoms of a more profound problem, the solution to which cannot come from outside in any form. The fundamental problem is a problem of the being which touches on the very essence of the African and can only be addressed by Africans themselves. There is a need for a new philosophy of life, not based on any alien political, ideological or economic philosophy, but that which emphasizes cross-cultural self-preserving ethical values and seeks to realign some of the spiritual energy of the African towards the improvement of interactions within the race as one unit. Development and African renaissance will come as a *fait accompli* when Africa consciously advances to this stage of relational energy management.

The Good Samafrican

The profligacy of Africa brings to mind an image of an African functionary playing host to a self-confessed inveterate liberal activist from the West whom he had accidentally met in the village administration office. The activist claimed that he had come to Africa to visit for a month. He was in the village for a week to *observe* the culture of the people.

The African functionary after listening to his story about how much he loved Africa and African peoples invited him over to stay in his house. The functionary, who lived in a two-bedroom house, with his wife, four children, two nephews and his mother welcomed him to his home. He moved out from the room which he shared with his wife and gave it to his newly found friend, exhorting him to feel at home. The African moved into the corridor with his wife, while the other members of the family crammed themselves into the sitting room. A new member had joined the family in the mind of the African host. The African host, whose pockets had been stretched before the arrival of his friend because of many mouths to feed and a savings towards a promised trip abroad soon went to his bank, exhausted all the family savings and borrowed money in order to be able to provide for the needs of his guest. He provided some stipend for the friend to buy his cigarettes and beer and for the occasional trip to the city. He would later find out that during these trips, the friend lodged in a good hotel in town, met with other friends from his country, drank excessively and was kept company by under-aged local girls. All inadvertently paid for by the functionary.

The Western *"friend"* stayed with the family for six months, eating well, sleeping under his own mosquito net because of African malaria, while the host and his family provided his share of dinner for mosquitoes. During the course of his stay, the activist prevailed on his African friend to secure permission for him from the elders of the village to visit the most sacred of shrines. He asked for sacred objects as gifts and bought some with money taken from his African friend. Under the guise of being alien to the local customs and culture, he walked half naked around the village (because it was too hot), barged in on solemn and sacred ceremonies, asked embarrassing questions to the consternation of the villagers, who quietly accepted these abominable eccentricities because, in their minds, he was a guest that should be treated with respect like all other guests. He took the tolerance accorded him by the villagers for acquiescent ignorance.

He finally left for his country, six months after arriving in the village.

A year later the African functionary was given a one-year scholarship by his community to study in his *friend's* country. This was his first time abroad, but he was quite confident that his friend would help him learn the ropes and probably provide for him in the same spirit as he had done when the friend was in his village. He was not overly concerned that he had spent all his savings towards this trip on his friend and all he had was a small contribution given to him by his community. He assured the community bank and other creditors that he would liquidate the debts incurred on hospitality on his return.

He was met by his friend at the airport and on the way to town the friend asked him the conditions of his scholarship. To this, the African explained that his tuition had been paid and he had been given some stipend for accommodation and feeding. The *friend* immediately proposed a students' hostel and he quickly added that there were many other students from Africa in this hostel. The African thanked him and asked if he could stay for a week with him and his family, just to learn how to go about things, before moving to the hostel. The *friend* explained that his wife would not be too happy with this arrangement and besides, his neighborhood was hostile to foreigners, particularly blacks; but he assured the African that he would certainly invite him over for dinner during the week. The activist dropped off his African friend at the hostel with a promise to be back in four days to have him over for dinner.

On the evening of his third day in the country, the African functionary decided to take a stroll in the neighborhood to buy some toiletries and familiarize himself with the area. On his way back, after making his purchases, he was attacked by a group of young people, whom he would later learn that they were called skinheads. He was physically harassed and his purchases and money were taken off him. Surprised and sad, the functionary returned to his hostel, nursed his bruises and passed the night without eating.

His activist *friend* came over the next day to take him over to his place for dinner. The activist lived in a three-bedroom apartment with his wife and their six year old daughter. He showed the African around the house: he and his wife shared a room, their daughter stayed in one, and the other they used for study and occasionally to practice playing African musical instruments. The functionary was surprised to find in his friend's apartment, an amazing collection of

all forms of ancient African art, including some which he had provided. After dinner, the functionary told his friend of his previous
day's ordeal and confessed that he needed some money. He
informed his friend and the wife of his debts at home and the difficulties of any chances of getting any immediate remittances from his
community.

Could his friend lend him some money? He quickly added that on
returning back to his village, he would immediately pay up this
loan.

The room became silent. The wife looked in horror at her husband.
A loaded pause of racing thoughts. A deafening silence. The African
became uncomfortable. His dark skin glistened with hot sweat of
shame shed by his trembling cells. He thought through what he had
said; had he committed some cultural abomination? The cells of his
mouth redirected their secretions to help the sweat glands of the
skin. His mouth was dry. He thought of telling his hosts that it was
all a joke; that he actually had money. Then he thought of the next
day, what would he eat? How would he survive in this foreign land?
He thought of informing his family, then remembered the still
unpaid debts incurred during the activist's visit the year before. He
could imagine the panic and the difficulties his family would face
back at home to raise money for him. A sudden image of him in the
streets of this strange country came into his mind. He had heard
that nothing could be taken on credit in this country; he could not
live on credit in the hostel, he could not buy books on credit. He
remembered the suspicious attitude of the Asian owner of the local
grocery shop, when he had gone there to make his purchases before
he was robbed. He dismissed as impossible any chances of getting
anything on credit from the shop; or any chances of survival without resorting to begging in the streets as he had seen some Africans

doing. He decided that he would rather beg his friend than face public humiliation.

The wife spoke first. Wordless speech carried in a leaden coffin of small cough. The trio came back to earth from their brief spell of celestial pilgrimage. The African was melting piece-meal. The heart was the first to go; the entrails then dropped in a tropical rain that inundated his village-made suit. His gods seemed far from this table.

His friend asked if he could speak with his wife in private for some moments. The functionary could only feebly nod, afraid that the bones in his neck were near to their melting point too and could give way. In the moments the couple was away, he thought of abandoning everything and going back to his village; then he thought of the shame this would spell for his family, the indignation of the local administration. Ideas tumbled and evaporated in his mind. He looked at the walls, fixed his eyes on a particular ancient carving which he had bought for his friend with a month's salary. He prayed to the devil form embedded in the carving.

The couple emerged shortly afterwards and smiled at him. He forced his melting mouth muscles into form, a caricature image of an intention of a smile.

The activist began with how much he loved Africa and Africans and how he was dedicated to helping them. He talked of demonstrations which he had led in the city. Marxism, Leninism, Pan Africanism, Negritude, IMF, World Bank, Fair trade, Unfair Commerce. The African was close to tears.

Finally he said that the African's request had caught them by surprise. He was sorry about the robbery and wished he could do something immediately. The family had been thinking of changing their furniture which they acquired a couple of years ago, and had been saving towards this. They had some other money saved, but that was for their vacation in a few months. But they would consider his request. Could he give them a week to think about his request? He could call back in about five days. The African reminded his friend that he did not even have money to phone. This drew a sigh from the wife, who rummaged through her purse and gave some coins. The couple announced that they had some other engagement and would go and drop him off in his hostel.

There were African students from *other-phone* countries living in the hostel. The African functionary tried to make friends with them. He hovered like a distant satellite around them hoping for some friendly contact. After all they were all foreigners here, and more importantly in his mind they were black Africans like him.

The *other-phones* ignored him.

He prayed the days would fly by so that he could contact his activist friend. The days crawled and he heard each hour toll in the rumbles of his empty stomach. Hunger, an alien being, for which they had no word in his language, became a faithful companion.

On the fifth day, he called his friend who appeared very happy to hear from him. His friend promised to pass by and see him. The functionary was full of expectations. He planned a revenge on those other Africans who had been ignoring him. When he got money from his friend, he would have a large feast all alone to himself right in the presence of those arrogant *other-phone* Africans.

The friend came in the company of another friend, whom he intro-duced as another friend of Africa, a fellow placard-carrying activist, an all-in-one embodiment of anti-globalization. This new friend was planning to visit the functionary's country and would like to visit his village. Could the African be kind to give him an introduc-tory letter to anyone in the village? They had come with pen and paper and the functionary quickly obliged them. It was smiles all round.

The African was expectant. He could almost see the envious faces of the other-phone Africans. He smiled and asked his friend about *"my humble request"*. The friend looked at the other friend of Africa, shrugged and said he was still working hard on being able to do something; there was the possibility that he could loan him some amount, not much, but on the condition that he paid back with prevailing bank interests. He explained why the interest was impor-tant. If the money remained in the bank, it would accrue some interests, which he and his wife had imputed into their budget for vacation. He explained the complexities of compound interests, which the functionary did not in any way understand, but was will-ing to agree to as long as he got some money. In order to guarantee the payment of the loan, the functionary's friend told him he had found him a night-guard job a few kilometers away, which though did not pay much would at least pay a part of his rent, leave some for a meal or two, and guarantee that the interest on the loan is paid.

The friend asked if the functionary would take the job. With no other options open, the functionary agreed. His friend warned him that the area was a bit dangerous. A notorious gangland, but if he would do his duty honestly by staying awake all night, he would be fine. The functionary confessed that this was going to be difficult, given that he had to study during the day. His friend advised him to tighten his belt, that nothing comes easy. "It is a win-win situation after all; you get a job, cater for your needs, you pay back my money and we remain friends".

The functionary later discovered from some complicated calculations presented to him at a later date by his friend that about seventy-five percent of his salary was going into paying the interest on the loan; the remaining twenty five percent was barely enough to buy him two meals a day and he was eventually expelled from his studies for poor performance.

Five years after, he was still over there, paying interests on the loan with no hope of ever getting the capital which seems to have grown through further complicated compound calculations. His recent calculation showed him that he had paid his activist friend more than five times what he originally borrowed.

He was fired from his night guard job. He wandered and slept in the streets for a period. He learnt how to beg in the streets. He learnt the art of rummaging in garbage bins for left-overs.

Fearful of default, the activist friend found him another job. The African functionary now works as a part-time cleaner of his friend's and other friends of Africa's apartments.

The functionary is now a very active member of the local church and mosque, where many like him, *other-phones,* gather on a regular basis to pray. They have prayed and fasted on several occasions for debt forgiveness. They talk of uniting to free themselves from their *master-friends*. However, because of the *historical ties* and their dependence, their intentions and resolutions are betrayed by their own members to their activists-friends.

The activists-friends have also constituted themselves into a club in order to protect their interests and investments.

Bibliography

1. Tariff Reform—Winston Churchill's Address to Textile Workers. Lancashire, 1909.

2. The Organization of African Unity Charter, Addis Ababa, 1963.

3. W.B. Yeats: The Second Coming

4. Henry Kissinger: Does America Need a Foreign Policy?

5. The Commission for Africa Report, March 2005

6. Georges Curvier: The Animal Kingdom, (1827–35),

7. Martin Meredith: Nelson Mandela, A Biography. Penguin Books 1997

8. Martin Meredith: Nelson Mandela, A Biography. Penguin Books 1997

9. Frantz Fanon. Wretched of the Earth. Penguin Books 2001.

10. Molefi Kete Asante: Afrocentricity: The Theory of Social Change.

11. General Charles de Gaulle's speech before Guinean parliament in his campaign for Guinean votes for The French Constitution of the Fifth Republic. 1958.

12. Agostinho Neto: Who is the enemy? What is our Objective? Speech. Dar es Salaam. 1974

13. Frantz Fanon. Wretched of the Earth. Penguin Books 2001.

14. John Mbiti: General Manifestation of African Religiosity.

15. Wole Soyinka: The Man Died. Spectrum Books. Ibadan, Nigeria. 2002.

16. Wole Soyinka: The Man Died. Spectrum Books. Ibadan, Nigeria. 2002.

17. W.E.B Du Bois: The Souls of Black Folk. Dover Thrift Editions. 1994

18. Fela Anikulapo Kuti: ITT (International Thief Thief) Musical.

19. Ottobah Cuguano: Narrative of the Enslavement of a Native of Africa. 1787.

20. Jean Barbot: A description of the coasts of north and south Guinea, and of Ethiopia…account of the Western maritime countries of Africa. 1732.

21. Ottobah Cuguano: Narrative of the Enslavement of a Native of Africa. 1787.

22. Alexander Falcolnbridge: An Account of the Slave Trade on the Coast of Africa.1788

23. Robert O. Collins: African History, text and readings, Random House. 1971

24. The Human Rights Watch: Background Paper on Slavery and Slavery Redemption in the Sudan. March 1999.

25. Georg Wilhelm Hegel: Philosophy of History.

26. Oruno Lara: Questions de Couleur: Blanches et Noires.1923

27. Yevgeny Chevchenko (Russian Poet): Lies. Poem.

28. Matt. T. Rosenberg: Berlin Conference of 1884–1885 to Divide Africa—The Colonization of the Continent by Colonial Powers. Article.

29. Commission for Africa Report. March 2005.

30. Agostinho Neto: Who is the enemy? What is our Objective? Speech. Dar es Salaam. 1974

31. Agostinho Neto: Who is the enemy? What is our Objective? Speech. Dar es Salaam. 1974

32. W.E.B Du Bois: The Souls of Black Folk. Dover Thrift Editions. 1994

33. Diedrich Westermann: Africa and Christianity. Oxford University Press, 1937.

34. Pope Paul VI: Africae Terrarum.1967

35. Pope John Paul II: Ecclesia in Africa

36. Robert O. Collins: African History, text and readings, Random House. 1971.

978-0-595-34819-0
0-595-34819-X